Renegade PAST⊘R'S GUIDE TO
TIME
MANAGEMENT

Dr. Nelson Searcy
& Richard Jarman

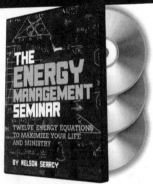

Library of Congress Cataloging-in-Publication Data
Searcy, Nelson
The Renegade Pastor's Guide to Time Management /
Nelson Searcy; with Richard Jarman
p. cm.
Includes bibliographical references.
ISBN: 978-0-9885241-9-4
1. Religion – Christian Ministry – Pastoral Resources

Printed in the United States of America
First Edition 2017

CONTENTS

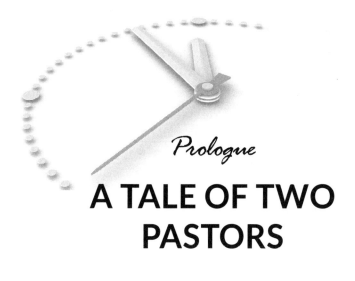

A TALE OF TWO PASTORS

Meet Joe Average. He is the pastor of First Community Church. Pastor Joe loves his church and gives all he can to help the people in his congregation fulfill their God-given potential. He has a wife, Jane, and three small children he adores. On a typical Monday Pastor Joe wakes up tired from a busy weekend of preaching, teaching, and reaching and heads to his weekly staff meeting. The staff of FCC is smart and dedicated to the mission of the church, but some staff members are frustrated because they feel as though Pastor Joe has trouble following through on his commitments. They often wonder whether he is spreading himself too thin.

Most weeks Pastor Joe can't find the time to set an agenda before the staff meeting, which means that the meeting inevitably runs long. Today that sets off a chain reaction, making him late for his next appointment, a lunch with some leaders of his denomination. At the end of the lunch meeting he commits to getting together with these leaders again the following week. He pulls out his phone and enters the appointment in his personal calendar but forgets to also put it on his work calendar when he gets back to the church. As a result he will later schedule a counseling session at church for the same time period as the lunch meeting. Oops.

Pastor Joe's typical week is filled with ordinary pastoral duties. He meets with church members and community leaders, teaches Bible studies, and prepares for the weekend worship services. He prides himself on responding to emails quickly, but that means that he checks his inbox over and over again throughout the course of a day. While online, he finds himself sucked into social media for far longer than he intends to be. Always short on time, Pastor Joe never has enough of that commodity to fully prepare for his sermons. He usually finishes preparing his message for Sunday on Saturday afternoon, even though Saturday is supposed to be his day off to spend with his family. In reality he hasn't taken a day off in months, except for the week he had to lie low thanks to a serious bout with the flu.

Pastor Joe is always running late, wherever he goes—including getting home to his family in the evening. Jane and the kids are accustomed to Joe's lateness or absence from family dinners and most family functions. They are understanding, justifying that his absence is just part of having a pastor for a husband and father. But Pastor Joe is frustrated that he doesn't get to spend as much time with his children as he would like. They are growing so fast, and he is missing many of their milestones. He also knows that his and Jane's relationship isn't quite what it should be, but he doesn't know—and can't seem to afford the time to grapple with—how to make it better.

Since he often misses dinner with his family, Pastor Joe ends up eating fast food on too many nights and rarely takes time for exercise. His weight keeps increasing every year, and he's starting to deal with some nagging health issues. He doesn't have the energy he used to and finds it harder and harder to drag himself out of bed each morning.

Pastor Joe loves being a pastor, but he wishes things could be different. He wants to be fully present and engaged in every situation. He longs to spend quality time with his family. He wants to be known as a leader who is calm, assured, and reliable. But he feels frazzled, as though he is being pulled in a thousand different directions, with no end in sight.

Sound familiar? Pastor Joe is living out the average pastor's experience ... but there is a better, healthier, and more productive way to operate. Let's take a look at another pastor's life.

Meet Rob Renegade. Pastor Rob is the pastor of Fellowship Church. His staff loves him. They admire his dependability and consistency. If he says he will do something, he does it. Staff members always receive agendas in advance of their meetings, and the meetings are productive and flow smoothly. Church members and community leaders also know they can rely on Pastor Rob. He maintains set office hours and rarely cheats his family by staying out later than anticipated.

Rob's wife, Rebecca, and his three kids are glad he is home most evenings. He gets to spend time watching his kids' school plays and sporting events. In addition, he enjoys a regular date night with his wife, and they feel closer to each other at this stage of life than ever before.

People who attend Fellowship Church regularly comment on how put-together Pastor Rob's sermons are. He sets aside time every week to prepare the message and consistently meets his own deadline of finishing by the end of the day on Thursday. In fact, he and his staff have the weekend service completely planned and ready to go each week by Thursday evening. This allows Pastor Rob to reserve Saturday as his Sabbath, a day in which he refrains from doing any church-related work. Instead, he spends his Saturday resting, recharging, and connecting with his loved ones. He is insanely busy, and his life as a pastor is stressful, but he knows he can handle whatever is thrown his way and looks forward to the future with confidence and hope.

With which pastor do you identify more: Joe or Rob? What if we were to ask it this way: Are you operating more in the realm of *average* or excellence? Most pastors we know feel more average than excellent. They are constantly being pushed one way, then pulled another. There is never enough time to accomplish everything they need to do. As a result, family time gets cut short. Sermon preparation is rushed. Physical health is neglected. Even though these pastors are engaged in a job they love—a job God has called them to—they end up feeling frustrated and burned out.

There is a better way. It is possible to manage your time so that you can stay on top of the never-ending demands of being a pastor, nurture your congregation, spend quality time with your family, and take care of your own physical and emotional needs. Are you ready to find out how? Read on.

Introduction

RENEGADE TIME MANAGEMENT

The fact that you are taking the time to read this book tells us one thing: you do not want to be an average pastor. You want to abandon average and strive for something greater. You want to be a renegade! A renegade pastor is one who has decided to live differently, to pursue godly excellence on every level, and to cultivate a life that most pastors will never experience—that of a pastor who has decided to reach his full potential in Christ for both his personal life and his ministry. If that's you, and we believe it is, welcome to the renegade club. You are in for an exciting journey!

Renegade pastors acknowledge that time is their most important resource, because there is only a finite amount of it. You can always make more money, but no matter how hard you work you can't make a day last longer than twenty-four hours. Average pastors don't use the resource of time wisely, and they pay the price emotionally, relationally, spiritually, and physically. Average pastors are overwhelmed with their commitments, become easily scattered and unfocused, and find that they have insufficient time for the most important things in life.

Renegade pastors are no less busy than average pastors (in fact, most are busier); they simply manage their days in such a way that they accomplish everything more effectively. They make and take time for family, time to rest, and time to take care of their bodies and minds. They are fruitful in their personal and professional lives. God blesses them with peace and productivity because they steward their time well. They weren't born knowing how to do this. They have simply adopted a set of principles that allows them to plan and execute their time with excellence. And you can do the same.

In this book you will learn many of the time management skills we have employed to make our own lives better, more peace-filled and effective. (We'll tell you a bit more about ourselves in just a minute.) As you implement the skills we will detail here, you will regain control of your time—and of your life. How can we be so sure? Because these very time-management principles have revolutionized our lives.

WHO WE ARE AND WHY WE WROTE THIS BOOK

Nelson Searcy — I (Nelson) am a pastor and church planter. I started The Journey Church in New York City, which now has several locations throughout New York City, as well as in Boca Raton, Florida. The Journey has consistently been on the list of America's fastest-growing churches. In addition, I am the founder of Church Leader Insights (www.ChurchLeaderInsights.com), which provides training and resources to help pastors and church leaders grow healthy churches. I have written more than fifteen books, both for church leaders and for a wider Christian audience. I have also personally coached several thousand pastors from all over the world through the Renegade Pastor's Network. After well over a decade in New York City, I currently live in Florida with my wife, Kelley, and my son, Alexander.

Richard Jarman — I (Richard) am the pastor of TouchPoint Church in Bell Gardens, California, just outside Los Angeles. My church is in one of the poorest areas of Southern California. TouchPoint is heavily involved in community ministry, helping the least fortunate with food, clothing, and survival skills. I have been married to my wife, Jennifer, for eighteen years, and we have five children. I have used, and continue to use, many of the time management skills we will discuss in this book to help me accomplish all that God has called me to do.

We both understand what it's like to be a pastor. We know the pressures and pains, as well as the joys and triumphs of leading a local church. And we know how the time-management principles in these pages can radically improve your life, just as they have improved ours. All you need to do is decide to abandon average. Choose to be a renegade when it comes to managing your time.

To be clear, we are not writing this book as experts who have solved every time management issue anyone will face. We remain learners on this journey, figuring out what works, rethinking our approach based on mistakes, and doing our best to make the most of that precious and elusive resource: time.

That means that we grapple with all the same struggles you do. It also means that we understand what you are going through as you work to change your habits and activities in ways that will help you maximize your time. Because we are still fighting the battle—though winning in many cases!—we are assured of one thing: with God's help you, too, can do this. You can be much better at managing your time than you are now. And the results are more than worth the work.

HOW TO READ THIS BOOK

The Renegade Pastor's Guide to Time Management contains thirty short principles to put you on the path to better time management. Most people have particular areas in which they struggle to manage their time, as well as areas in which they do well. We recommend that you start by reading the chapters that relate to your weakest areas. Each chapter is self-contained, so you don't have to read them in the order presented.

That said, we encourage you to read and begin applying one principle every day over a thirty-day period. At the end of one month you will be managing your time much better than when you started. With many of these tips you will see immediate time savings and near-instantaneous productivity gains. With others it will take a few days or even weeks to see the full effect of the changes. Either way, know that your diligent effort will make a huge difference in your ministry and in your life.

Here's a bold claim we are willing to stand behind: **if you implement any of the ideas in this book, you can save up to one hour every week. By implementing all of these ideas, you could save an extra thirty-one hours each month.**

The more of these ideas you apply the more time you will save. That means more time for the mission to which God has called you; more time with your family; and an enhanced reputation, both for yourself as a leader and for your church. We are confident that God will use the tips, principles, and skills you find here to help you fulfill every purpose he has in store for you.

We believe that pastors have the most important job in the world. People's lives and eternal destinies are changed by what we allow God to do through us. When we learn to manage our time wisely, we are preparing for God to use us to make an even bigger impact for his glory.

Are you ready to go renegade?

Chapter 1

MAKE TIME
MANAGEMENT FUN

Management is not a word that gets most people excited. It carries the idea of preserving something, of maintaining the status quo, of disallowing a situation to spiral out of control. Or, as in the case of time management, it can simply mean attempting to handle something more effectively. While important, the term doesn't make you want to jump up and do something.

This connotation may be one of the reasons time management isn't considered an exciting topic—even though the results of good time management are exciting and often life-changing. Besides, learning to manage time more effectively can be hard work, work that shoves us beyond the perimeters of our comfort zones. It involves not only learning but also internalizing new skills, breaking old habits, and making new practices a part of your daily routine. Given all of this, it's easy to see why a busy average pastor may not want to seriously consider what it would take to manage time more effectively. But the renegade pastor understands how revolutionary good time management can be and jumps at the chance to see its results in his life and ministry.

Time is arguably the most valuable single resource at our disposal. And it's the only resource you can't make more of. Once a moment is gone, it is gone forever—whether or not you have spent

15

it wisely. That's why it's so vital to make the most of this precious gift God has given you, to learn to the very best of your ability how to optimize the minutes and hours that make up your days.

Because it can be difficult to learn new time management skills and replace old habits with better ones, you must keep yourself consistently motivated to do so. One way to do this is to make time management a game.

WHY TO MAKE TIME MANAGEMENT A GAME

When you were a kid, games were an important part of learning. You learned how to interact with other people by playing with them. You learned how to play baseball or basketball or some other sport through playing it. But as you and I got older, many of us stopped playing—which is a shame. We learn things so much more quickly and effectively when we're having fun.

Learning the principles and skills of time management is no exception. The benefits of making a game of time management include:

- *Making time management enjoyable.* You are more likely to stick with something when you enjoy doing it. So why not learn to enjoy time management?

- *Helping you be more creative with the application of new skills and techniques.* You learn best when your mind is free to create and connect in different ways. When time management is a game, you can be more creative and increase your capacity for learning.

- *Allowing you to get other people involved in the learning.* People are more likely to help you with fun activities than with tasks they see as tedious or boring. Turning time management into a game encourages other people to also get involved in the fun of learning to manage time.

- *Giving you a new approach for learning familiar skills.* You may already know many of the things you need to do to manage your time more effectively—you just haven't done them yet. Instead of seeing these things as chores or necessities, approach them as a great opportunity for learning.

SIX WAYS TO MAKE TIME MANAGEMENT FUN

Turning time management into a game can be fun and rewarding. Not only will doing so make these skills much easier to learn, but it will help you to internalize them, to integrate what you have learned into your daily life. Here are six tips that will help you have fun with this serious endeavor:

1. *Change your way of thinking.* You may think you are too busy for games—but the reality is that you're too busy *not* to participate in the game of time management.

2. *Challenge yourself.* See whether you can accomplish certain activities more quickly as you incorporate the tips in this book. Chart your progress so you can know when you are moving forward. Compare multiple approaches to determine which are faster and more effective. When you hit upon a good way to do something, double down and try to do it even better.

3. *Compete with others.* Find other pastors who also want to better themselves and initiate some friendly competition. Try to outdo each other with your levels of efficiency and effectiveness. Too many pastors compete over issues like attendance and budgets. Let those go and start competing over something that can make your respective ministries healthier and more fruitful.

4. *Expect setbacks.* Progress comes with repetition and practice. Don't be too hard on yourself when you are trying a new time management game and lose a round. Keep working at it. The improvement will come.

5. *Celebrate progress.* Time management involves a never-ending cycle of improvement. There isn't a finish line; like the athlete continuously striving to break a previous record, you can always do better. Don't wait till you achieve some nebulous standard of perfection; instead, celebrate your incremental successes. Reward yourself for making progress in any area.

6. *Get a cheering section.* No sporting event would be complete without fans going crazy for their favorite team. Gather some people who will intentionally celebrate with you when you make even a small amount of progress. Their encouragement will go a long way.

Effective time management will drastically improve your life. Learning to incorporate the principles and skills it requires should be a fun experience, not a painful or laborious one. Decide to start thinking of your time management journey as a game. Compete against yourself. Compete against others. Celebrate your victories. Have some fun as you change your life for the better!

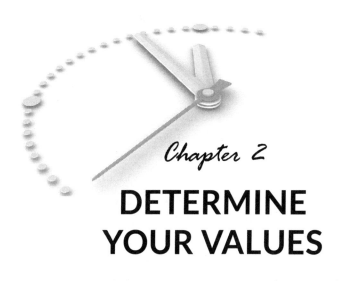

Chapter 2

DETERMINE YOUR VALUES

Pastors are a remarkable group of people. They are smart, hardworking, and passionate. They love God and care deeply about others. But as capable as they are, there is one thing that even pastors can't do: they cannot create more time. Like everyone else in the world, they are bound within the confines of the twenty-four-hour day.

Since there are a limited number of hours available to us, you and I need to make sure we take full advantage of each one. It isn't enough to be able to do things faster. We must know how to do the *right* things faster.

What are those right things? That will be determined by your values. Renegade pastors are intentional about investing their time in a way that aligns with their values—about avoiding the proverbial tyranny of the urgent and expending the bulk of their time and energy engaged in the things that matter most to them. To determine your values you simply need to ask yourself, "What is most important to me?"

DIFFERENT PEOPLE, DIFFERENT VALUES

It goes without saying that some areas should be important to all Christians. We should all value obeying God, spending time in God's

Word and in prayer, and reaching the lost. But the time-management values we are talking about will be different for every believer.

There is an amazing amount of diversity in humanity—including, of course, within the body of Christ. God has created each of us to do different things. In Ephesians 2:10 the apostle Paul writes, "We are God's masterpiece. He has created us anew in Christ Jesus, so we can do the good things he planned for us long ago."

What a phrase: "We are God's masterpiece"! Just think about that. God forms each of his children in a unique way, different from everyone else in the world. And his purpose for doing this? "So we can do the good things he planned for us long ago." Since God has called each of us to do different things, we will consider different things important. In other words, we will each value different things.

HOW TO DETERMINE YOUR VALUES

How can you determine exactly what God has called you to accomplish—and, consequently, which issues and principles are most important to you? The following five questions will help you define your values:

1. *What makes you happiest?* I (Richard) am not an accountant. While I understand church and personal budgeting to the extent I need to, I have no desire to spend my time crunching numbers. But I know others who love numbers. Their happiest hours are spent digging into the details of church or personal finances. They've been blessed with a love for financial minutiae and called to operate effectively in that area. You can often determine what God would have you focus on by looking at what makes you happiest.

2. *What are you good at?* While it's true that God stretches us by calling us to minister in areas in which we are weak, he also delights in using our strengths for his glory. What particular skills do you possess that God may be able to use? What comes easily to you, particularly in an area in which many of your ministry colleagues may struggle? The areas in which you are most interested and competent are likely those in which God is calling you to operate.

3. *What makes you angry?* In what areas do you experience what Bill Hybels calls "holy discontent"? There are likely situations that drive you crazy, even though others around you may shrug them off or take them in stride. If something consistently annoys you, God may be calling you to focus your attention there and make the situation better. He opens our eyes to glitches, hitches, and hiccups, minor as they may seem, because he wants us to help make it right.

4. *What makes you feel most fulfilled or satisfied?* This is similar to the question about what makes you happiest. Are there certain activities or areas of your work—whether easier or more difficult—that cause you to experience a particular sense of fulfillment or satisfaction? For example, I (Richard) derive great fulfillment from working with kids in foster care. I (Nelson) get similar satisfaction from coaching pastors and church leaders. Focus on those areas that make you feel most fulfilled.

5. *What would you like your legacy to be?* When you come to the end of your life, what do you want people to say about you? What do you want them to say about your life's achievements? We all want to make an impact—where

do you want your impact to be made? The areas that come to mind when you consider this question are likely the ones to which God is calling you.

Take some time to answer those five questions prayerfully, asking God for wisdom. As you do, you will likely notice common themes emerging. Let these themes guide you as you identify and consider your values. Allow them to help you clarify what's most important to you. Then be intentional about focusing your time and attention on the areas that best align with what you've discovered. As you work through this process you will become more intentional about planning your days, weeks, months, and years in ways that will allow you to invest quality time on the things you highly value.

When you invest in the areas that are of the highest value to you, you will find yourself operating with:

- Greater satisfaction in your work

- Greater impact for the Kingdom of God

- The ability to work with greater passion

- Greater focus on the particular things God has called you to do

One brief note about determining your values: you should repeat this exercise at different points throughout your life, as a way of seeing whether God is keeping you where you are or steering you into a new area of focus. As the years go by God may call you to concentrate on different areas. Renegade pastors stay open to his leading, intentionally focusing their attention in whatever direction he points them.

Chapter 3

BE BOTH EFFICIENT AND EFFECTIVE

In October of 1964 Minnesota Vikings defensive lineman Jim Marshall picked up a fumble during a game against the San Francisco 49ers. Marshall looked up, saw a clear path to the end zone, and took off, hoping to score a touchdown. But when he made it to the victory line he realized that he had run sixty yards in the wrong direction. Instead of scoring six points for his team, he had managed to score two for the opponents.

Marshall had done everything efficiently. He had scooped up the football in one seamless motion and had hurtled straight and fast toward the end zone. Still, his efforts weren't effective. Marshall's blunder, often cited as one of the worst plays in the history of the National Football League, illustrates a classic truth: you can be very efficient without being effective at all.

Can you relate to Wrong-Way Jim? Most pastors can. Too often it is extraordinarily difficult for us to get, and remain, focused on what we should be doing. Instead we end up running in directions that seem right but don't get us any closer to the end goal God has laid out for us. Renegade pastors must be intentional, not just about working diligently but about working diligently at the things that matter most.

Many time-management resources focus on how to become more efficient—teaching you how to get things done competently and quickly, without expending wasted effort. While we are going to cover some keys to efficiency in these pages, we are also committed to helping you figure out *what* it is that you should be doing so efficiently. As Peter Drucker once noted, "Efficiency is doing things right. Effectiveness is doing the right thing." We want you to be both efficient and effective for God's Kingdom.

THE IMPORTANCE OF BEING EFFICIENT

Efficiency is vital in any business—and in any church. In a church setting it translates into better stewardship of God's resources. Inefficiency is wasteful and even sinful in that it squanders the three most important resources God gives us: time, money, and people. Time gets wasted doing things in ways that need to be improved upon, streamlined, or updated. Money given to us by churchgoers or financial partners gets wasted on initiatives that aren't the most critical. And other people get frustrated when they realize that their time and money aren't being well utilized.

Many churches operate on the basis of habit. Things are done the way they have always been done, without looking at why they are—or were originally—done in that way or whether there might be a better way to accomplish the same goals. Efficiency is an afterthought, if it is a thought at all. That leads to average results—or worse. Any time you and I can institute procedures that will help us make better use of the resources God has given us, we should do so. Renegade pastors must be committed to making sure we are as efficient as we can be in every area of leadership.

To begin moving toward greater efficiency, ask yourself (and the other leaders in your church) these important questions:

- Do we conduct too many meetings or appoint too many committees?

- Is there a way to do things more cost-effectively?

- Are the right people in the right positions?

- Do we offer settings in which staff members can work quietly and uninterrupted?

- Do we have automated systems in place wherever possible? (For more on setting up healthy church systems, visit ChurchLeaderInsights.com.)

These questions can help you identify key areas in which the efficiency level can be raised in your church.

HOW TO BE MORE EFFECTIVE

As important as efficiency is, effectiveness is even more important. Effectiveness is the byproduct of working efficiently on the right things. In the world of church leadership, greater effectiveness comes through achieving more of what God has called your church to do and be—and that starts with you. Your church's effectiveness will to a large degree reflect your personal effectiveness. If your church sees you focused on the things God has given you to do, they will be more engaged in the vital mission of the church. On the other hand, if they see you caught up in unimportant activities, they too will get lost in minutia. As goes the pastor, so goes the church.

How do you increase the effectiveness of your church? How do you ensure that your church is engaged in accomplishing the mission God has given it? Here are a few ideas:

- *Make sure your church is clear on its mission and vision.* Does your church know why it exists? Many church members don't understand why the local church is so important. Preach often on the reason God has placed you where you are, until this is ingrained in the hearts of your members.

- *Regularly evaluate the activities of your church.* Again, too many churches do things a certain way just because they always have. Don't be that kind of church. Be willing to honestly evaluate what your church is doing, and why, in every area of ministry. Make sure everything you do helps to advance your church's mission.

- *Pray consistently.* Stay connected to God. It is easy to get so busy that you forget that running a church is a spiritual work. Ask God for the wisdom to know what to do, the courage to do what you should, favor on all your interactions, and fruit from your ministry.

- *Budget according to your values.* Make sure you have money designated for the things you say you care about. No church has enough money for everything, so work to ensure that the important things are covered.

- *Focus on people, not programs.* Reaching and discipling people are key to solving the most pressing problems most churches encounter. Focus on establishing relationships with people—on seeing them come to and grow in Jesus.

When you are engaged in these activities, you will see an increase both in your personal effectiveness and in the effectiveness of your church.

Chapter 4

CHOOSE IMPORTANT OVER URGENT

Remember Pastor Joe Average? He's a busy man. He stays on top of everything that is happening at First Community Church. When something goes wrong he makes certain it gets fixed. When someone writes a negative email to the church, he personally answers it. He prides himself on how he handles each crisis that pops up.

Here's the problem: Pastor Joe is so busy taking care of day-to-day urgencies that he has little time or energy left to focus on the things that matter most to the church. Sermon preparation often takes a back seat to more pressing matters, as does following up with first-time guests. He wishes he could do things differently, but he's just not sure how to make that happen.

Can you empathize with Pastor Joe? Do you feel pulled in too many different and even conflicting directions or see yourself as responsible for personally handling every problem that arises? Do you spend more time putting out fires than concentrating on God's ultimate vision for you church? If so, you are not alone.

SPENDING TIME IN THE CORRECT QUADRANT

Answering angry emails. Meeting with disgruntled staff. Calling a plumber to fix a broken pipe. These are all urgent activities. They need attention right away. Someone must handle them. In the meantime, other activities vital to the health and growth of the church—like sermon preparation, new guest follow-up, personal devotions, and vision casting, to name a few—often get pushed aside. One of the keys renegade pastors use to effectively manage their time is to be intentional about spending more time concentrating on the important things of ministry, while limiting the time spent putting out ministry fires.

In his classic work *The 7 Habits Of Highly Effective People*, Stephen Covey writes about the importance of understanding the four quadrants of time. The quadrants look something like this:

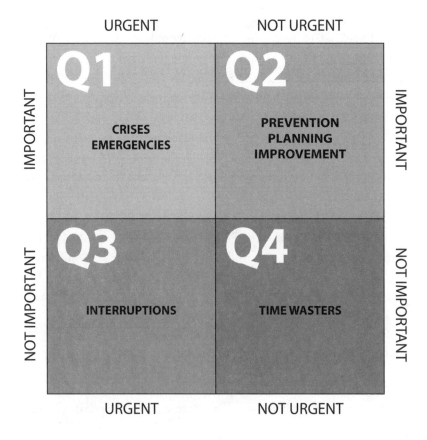

Quadrant 1 tasks are those things that are both urgent and important: a family member develops a sudden illness and you need to go to the hospital, or a busted pipe is flooding the church basement. These issues require immediate attention. But things that are both important and urgent are relatively rare.

Quadrant 2 tasks and activities are those things that are truly important in the long term: coaching and personal improvement, assimilating new members, strategic planning, personal devotions, and the like. These things won't jump up and down demanding your attention, but you would be wise to focus your energy on them regularly.

Quadrant 3 is reserved for legitimate interruptions, and quadrant 4 is a dumping ground for those things that simply waste your time. Covey contends that, in order to be effective, you need to spend more time in Quadrant 2 and less in Quadrants 1, 3, and 4. When you pour your time and energy into what's truly important, while still taking care of the occasional emergency, you will be a better, more effective leader—and your church will benefit from the difference.

THE DIFFERENCE BETWEEN QUADRANTS 2 AND 3

Most pastors don't waste a lot of time. They don't spend work hours watching movies or playing solitaire. But the majority do struggle to find the best ways to invest their time. The biggest dilemma most pastors face is determining what belongs in Quadrant 2 versus what belongs in Quadrant 3. What's the best way to recognize whether something is really important, as opposed to merely urgent?

To begin with, something is urgent when it must be done right now. Something is important when it contributes to your own or your church's long-term health and happiness. The problem is that when something needs immediate attention it can seem very important. Often, however, we determine in hindsight that the urgent situation was not that important in the long run.

So how can a renegade pastor get good at determining whether an activity falls into Quadrant 2 or Quadrant 3—whether it is important (in some cases also urgent) or merely urgent? Start by asking yourself these questions:

- *What's important to me?* (See Chapter 2: "Determine Your Values.") If you haven't assessed what's truly important to you, it will be difficult to determine how you should invest your time. Settle in your own mind and heart what God has called you to do, and then plan your time accordingly.

- *Is there a deadline on this activity?* Sometimes an activity is urgent because it needs to be completed by a certain time. For example, if you receive a job offer and need to respond in a timely manner, or if you need to finish a book you are writing. Deadlines make an activity inherently more urgent.

- *Will this activity build an important relationship?* Date night is a great example of an activity that builds an important relationship—but is easy to put off in favor of spending time on more pressing matters. Allow us to encourage you to make time for a regular date night with your spouse. This is not just important but vital to your relationship.

- *Will this activity clarify or enlarge the vision of our church?* One of the more important things every pastor should do is cast a compelling vision for his church. Of course, this is not urgent. But it is important and necessary. Make time for it.

- *Will this activity make me better emotionally, spiritually, mentally, or physically?* You may not see the immediate impact of a daily quiet time or physical exercise. But over time you will pay the price for not doing such things. That makes them extremely important.

- *Will this activity pay dividends for the church (or for my family) in the future?* Planning rarely seems urgent, but the old saying rings true: if you fail to plan, you are planning to fail.

THE BENEFIT OF STAYING IN QUADRANT 2

Learning to spend most of your time in Quadrant 2 can take some work, but it will bring you countless benefits. You will find yourself more effective, more fulfilled, and less stressed. You will also discover that the more time you spend on Quadrant 2 activities the fewer urgent activities (Quadrants 1 and 3) you will need to deal with.

Why? The planning that goes on in Quadrant 2 heads off many crises that come up due to a lack of planning. When you devote time to building relationships, for example, you spend less of it trying to repair fractured or strained ones. When you consistently clarify or remind others of the vision of your church, you will have more excited people to delegate Quadrant 3 tasks to. As a renegade pastor you will come to realize that working in Quadrant 2 actually gives you more time—time you can invest in tasks that are valuable and satisfying.

Chapter 5

PRAY THE TIME MANAGEMENT PRAYER

As a pastor, you are no doubt familiar with the many prayers found in the Bible. There is the Model Prayer that Jesus gave his disciples. The apostle Paul writes about the prayers he prayed for the churches that received his letters. And many of the Psalms are in the form of prayers. The prayer of the biblical figure Jabez became the focus of a best-selling book several years ago.

There is another prayer that, though not specifically found in the Bible, is vital for every renegade pastor. In fact, this is a prayer God can use to revolutionize your life. It's short and simple—just one easy-to-remember line. Are you ready? Here it is:

God, what is the best use of my time right now?

God is happy to answer this little prayer when you and I ask him sincerely. At its core, it is a prayer for wisdom. In James 1:5 Jesus' brother writes, "If you need wisdom, ask our generous God and he will give it to you. He will not rebuke you for asking." When you and I ask God what is the best use of our time, we are simply asking him for wisdom on how to shape our days. As James writes, God is generous and will be happy to give us an answer.

Time management isn't merely a good leadership skill. For renegade pastors, it's a spiritual discipline. The local church pastor has the most important job in the world—and time is the most important resource God gives each of us. As such, our time needs to be used in the most effective way possible. Only God truly knows what that means for each of us.

Praying this Time Management Prayer is an act of faith. You are trusting that God knows and wants what is best for you. This prayer shows God that you are open to his will day by day. We have seen God answer this prayer many times in our own lives and are confident that he will answer it in yours.

WHY YOU SHOULD PRAY THE TIME MANAGEMENT PRAYER

Most average pastors don't pray the Time Management Prayer. They are content to ask God for general direction. But renegade pastors acknowledge their need for God's specific direction every moment of every day. When you begin praying this prayer, you will see many blessings showing up in your life. Here are two of the greatest:

- *You will be able to do everything with greater conviction.* Whether you are leading a staff meeting or playing football with your kids, you will be able to immerse yourself in the moment, knowing that you are exactly where God wants you to be. This prayer frees you to enjoy the present.

- *You will be able to do everything with greater passion.* When you know you are doing exactly what God wants you to do, you can engage with your whole heart.

What pastor doesn't need more conviction and passion in his life? That's what this prayer will give you.

BEFORE YOU PRAY THE TIME MANAGEMENT PRAYER

Before you pray, there are a few things you need to have settled in your heart and mind:

- *Pray, expecting God to answer.* When you ask God for wisdom, ask with a sense of certainty that he will answer your prayer (James 1:6). Be on the lookout for God to move in response to this prayer. He will.

- *Pray, ready to obey God, no matter how he responds.* There is no use asking God which way to move if you have no intention of moving. God doesn't give us his wisdom for our own information; he gives it to guide us in the way he wants us to go. Make sure you "pray with your running shoes on," as we like to say.

- *Pray over your values.* As discussed in Chapter 2, be sure to spend some time clarifying your values in your heart and mind. When God directs you, it will likely be along the lines of one of these core values. In answering your prayer he will make use of the way he has wired you.

- *Pray specifically.* We have all heard people ask God to bless everybody in the world or to feed all the hungry people. While those prayers may be well intentioned, renegade pastors pray prayers that require a more specific answer. God operates in the details—just look at the magnificence of creation for proof. He is willing to give you a detailed answer to your prayer—if you are willing to listen and accept it.

WHEN TO PRAY THE
TIME MANAGEMENT PRAYER

When should you pray this prayer? The short answer is any time you need wisdom about how to use your time. But we have found it particularly helpful to pray this prayer at specific times:

- *At the beginning of every day.* Start your day by meditating on God's Word and talking with him in prayer. Make the Time Management Prayer part of this morning devotion.

- *During natural transitions throughout the day.* Every day has natural transition points—breaks, meals, a few minutes of down time after an appointment, etc. During these times ask God to lead and direct you.

- *When planning your calendar for the week ahead.* Make planning your calendar an exercise of faith by praying for wisdom with regard to every activity.

- *During interruptions.* Interruptions can be huge time-wasters. Ask God to show you which interruptions are unnecessary—and which are actually divine appointments.

If you pray the Time Management Prayer in faith, expecting God to answer, he will. This one practice will have a great impact on the shape and quality of your days.

Chapter 6

OUTLINE YOUR IDEAL DAY

What would a perfect day look like for you? Would it be a day spent with your family? Would you invest your morning in helping with a big evangelistic outreach? Maybe you would preach multiple times to packed audiences. The answer will be different for each of us because God has created us all so uniquely.

Perhaps you aren't sure how you would answer that question. Maybe you've never considered what a perfect day might look like. Most people haven't. You are likely so busy with everything you need to do that the thought of stepping back and visualizing a hypothetical perfect day seems like a waste of time. After all, who has time to daydream about a fictional day when actual days are filled with so much activity and responsibility?

THE IMPORTANCE OF OUTLINING YOUR IDEAL DAY

Taking the time to outline what an ideal day would look like for you is in reality a worthwhile exercise—and a simple one. Just ask yourself what you would do in any given twenty-four-hour period if you could do anything you wanted. Don't worry about money or other resources or restrictions. Simply think about what you would do with yourself if offered the chance to craft a perfect day. Answering this question will not be time wasted. In fact, it might be a catalyst for discovering how to invest your time more wisely, in things that will really make a difference.

This exercise, which has been utilized for decades by many of the most successful people in every field, is an important one. By engaging it you will find out a lot about who God has created you to be and what you want out of life. You will see many resulting benefits, including:

- *Greater clarity.* As you picture your ideal day, those things that are most important to you will rise to the surface. God put you on Earth for a reason. On your ideal day you will want to spend time invested in an area in which he has particularly qualified you.

- *Recognition of areas needing improvement.* When you consider what you would do on an ideal day, you will also gain some clarity on what you should stop doing.

- *Increased energy.* As you rediscover and deliberately invest in the things that matter most to you, you will feel your passion reigniting—a definite energy booster.

HOW TO OUTLINE YOUR IDEAL DAY

Are you beginning to see how valuable this exercise can be? When you're ready to do it for yourself, block out some time, being sure to remove yourself from all distractions. You will need space to think and pray. As you begin to sketch out your ideal day, keep these guidelines in mind:

1. *Be specific.* Describe where and when you will wake up. Describe what kind of food you will eat. Describe the kind of physical exercise you will do. This kind of detail will begin providing clarity on what you really want.

2. *Note the people with whom you will be interacting.* You don't live your life alone, so be careful not to craft a day of isolation. With whom will you be working? Spending quality personal time?

3. *Include both family and ministry activities.* What would you do with your family on an ideal day? On what kind of ministry would you focus? Again, be specific.

4. *Consider what excites you.* God has wired you so that certain things stir your heart. Let those things inform your ideal day.

5. *Conduct this exercise more than once.* Most likely you will miss something or forget something important the first time around. Wait a week, do it again (without consulting your earlier notes), and compare your results. Your perfect day will lie somewhere in the combination of the two efforts.

Here's a bonus tip to help you plan your day:

6. *Bathe this exercise in prayer.* More than anything else, outlining your ideal day is a spiritual exercise. It should stretch your faith and clarify your mission. Ask God for wisdom, insight, and courage. And don't forget to thank him when he answers your prayer.

Allow yourself to take a breather and enjoy this exercise. It will infuse your life and ministry with renewed excitement. You will rediscover that little flame that God originally lit in you—the one that may have been slightly dampened by everyday chaos and demands—and you'll be able refocus on exactly what he wants for your life. Yes, the exercise may be a little time consuming, but it will in the long run be time well spent.

Chapter 7

KEEP THE SABBATH

I (Nelson) will never forget the day I was called a sinner and told to repent. I had been the pastor of The Journey Church for four years. We were a large, growing church, and I was tired. I was overwhelmed. I was frustrated by all I had to do. My to-do list was constantly growing. My health was slipping. To be honest, my marriage wasn't all that great either. And I hadn't had a day off in ages.

I was on my monthly phone call with one of my mentors, complaining about everything that was going wrong in my life. I was hoping for some sympathy, but my mentor gave me what I needed rather than what I wanted. He told me bluntly, "Nelson, you're a sinner—and not just an ordinary one. You are a major sinner and you need to repent. You are violating the Ten Commandments!" He pointed out that every problem I was complaining about was a direct result of violating the Fourth Commandment and that I needed to stop that violation right away. Even though this was hardly what I wanted to hear, I took his words to heart. Now I can honestly say that my mentor's direct encouragement to begin keeping the Sabbath changed my life. It will change yours as well.

A LIFE-CHANGING PRINCIPLE

What is a Sabbath? It's a weekly twenty-four-hour period dedicated exclusively to resting and recharging. This can be any twenty-four hours during the week. During your Sabbath day you should intentionally stay away from anything work-related and use your time to reconnect with God and your family and to do things that refresh your soul. In order for you to remain effective in the long term, you *must* take a Sabbath day of rest. It's non-negotiable, and it isn't an indulgence. Both of us see this as so important that we both keep a weekly Sabbath—and require our staff members to do the same!

Of course, the most important reason to keep the Sabbath is that God commands it:

> *Remember to observe the Sabbath day by keeping it holy.*
> *You have six days each week for your ordinary work, but the seventh*
> *day is a Sabbath day of rest dedicated to the LORD your God.*
> (Exodus 20:8–10)

As pastors, you and I need to set an example of obedience for our churches to follow. When we observe a weekly Sabbath we are a walking sermon on the importance of doing what God commands.

THE PRACTICAL BENEFITS OF THE SABBATH

If obedience to God were the only reason to observe a Sabbath, that would be enough. But obedience is not the only reason. There are many practical benefits to keeping a weekly Sabbath. Here are just a few of them:

- *Your to-do list will no longer feel overwhelming.* It won't get any shorter, but you will finally feel in control of it. Keeping a Sabbath forces you to put a deadline on everything you need to do. You'll do your daily work within the framework of the reality that once your Sabbath comes everything needs to either be finished or put on hold—no ifs, ands, or buts. God himself modeled for you the need for a Sabbath rest, and he'll get along just fine while you recharge!

- *You will get better at prioritizing throughout the week.* When your work week set at six-day days, you know you need to spend those days focused on the most important items on your agenda.

- *You will enjoy a much more fulfilling family life.* Your decision to set aside a day to invest in your family will speak volumes to them (as well as to watching others) about how much they matter to you. The ongoing benefits of that realization will be life- and family-changing and will inevitably set an example for your congregation and community.

- *Your stress level will go down and your physical wellbeing will improve.* As your stress decreases you will likely make better health choices, perhaps losing some weight and getting into better physical shape. Your improved health will result in renewed energy; sharper focus; a more rounded personal profile; and, ultimately, a more fruitful ministry.

- *Keeping a weekly Sabbath will make you more productive.* A recent story in the *Harvard Business Review* detailed a study showing that professionals who took a regular, planned day off accomplished more overall than those who didn't plan an off day into their schedules. We often liken this to the principle of tithing. As pastors we know that when people tithe, the remaining 90% of their income stretches farther than the full un-tithed 100% would. In the same way, when you commit to taking a day to rest and recharge, you will accomplish more on the other six days of the week than if you had worked all seven.

MAKING THE MOST OF YOUR SABBATH

The benefits of observing a weekly Sabbath cannot be overstated. This is an essential practice for any pastor who wants to wisely manage his time, ministry, and family life. If you aren't currently taking a Sabbath, please trust us and give it a try. You'll be amazed by how following God's prescription for rest—even he took a day off after working six—can revolutionize your life. Here are a few ideas about how make the most of your Sabbath:

- *Block it out on your calendar every week.* This may be the most important single thing you do. If you don't make your Sabbath a part of your schedule, it will get crowded out by other, more urgent things. Decide which day will be your Sabbath and stick to it, no matter what.

- *Enlist your staff in helping you keep your Sabbath.* Let everyone who works with you know that you will not be available on that day.

- *Ensure that your staff members also keep a weekly Sabbath.* Everyone needs it. We suggest making Sabbath observance mandatory.

- *Inform your family of your plan to take a weekly Sabbath.* They will appreciate what you're doing. Let them hold you accountable for keeping your commitment.

- *Guard your Sabbath as though your life depends on it— because it does.* Don't let anything usurp your day of rest.

God gave us the gift of the Sabbath for our own good. We are called to follow his example, work hard at what he has called us to the other six days, and then take the time we need to rest and renew our reserves. We don't have time not to.

Chapter 8

GET UP ONE HOUR EARLIER

I (Nelson) love to get up early. I find that by waking up early, I get more done. Often I write first thing in the morning, immediately after my daily quiet time. When I do, I can knock out a lot of the writing I want to get done before most people have even started their day.

I (Richard), on the other hand, am not a morning person. I am much more comfortable staying up very late and then getting up late the next day. But over the years I have learned the value of training myself to get up earlier. With five active kids I need to get up early just to stay ahead of them. So now, for the first time in my life, I can consider myself—out of necessity—a morning person.

THE VALUE OF GETTING UP EARLIER

Renegade pastors should wake up earlier than most other people. Being early to rise is an important component for accomplishing everything to which God is calling you—daily, over the longer term, and ultimately. Following are some of the benefits you can expect when you make getting up early a habit in your life:

- *Health*: Studies show that early risers are healthier than night owls. Your ministry is far too important for you to waste time being sick.

- *Happiness*: Early risers are typically happier people. This is especially true for those who incorporate both exercise and quiet reflection into their morning routine. In fact, getting up early might be one of the most beneficial things you can do for your mental and emotional health.

- *Success*: Waking up early can help you be more successful in life and ministry. The list of successful early risers is long and impressive. From John Wesley to J. C. Ryle, in the Christian sphere, to Richard Branson and Apple CEO Tim Cook, many extremely successful individuals extoll the virtues of getting up early.

- *Time*: Early risers have more time to spend with family. This is especially important if you have kids at home. Getting up early gives you time to spend with your kids before school and/or with your wife before work. And since you'll have more daytime hours to get your work done, you may find that you also have more time in the evenings to be home—and otherwise present!—with your family.

When you combine the benefits to mind, body, and spirit, it just makes sense for renegade pastors to be intentional about waking up early.

HOW TO DEVELOP THE HABIT OF WAKING UP EARLIER

The question becomes *How do I do it?* Maybe you already get up reasonably early. If that's the case we believe you can benefit from waking up even earlier. If you are accustomed to sleeping in, you will see huge benefits from developing this habit. (It goes without saying that a reasonably early bedtime must fit into the equation as well. More on this to follow.)

Start by committing to wake up one hour earlier than you are accustomed to. This will take discipline. Here are nine tips for getting out of bed and adding this extra hour to your day.

1. *Build up fifteen minutes at a time.* Instead of just waking up an hour earlier, start by setting your alarm to go off fifteen minutes earlier tomorrow morning. Do that for a week and then get up fifteen minutes earlier than that during the next week. Do this until you are regularly up an hour earlier. This will make the transition much easier.

2. *Never use your snooze button.* We are convinced that the snooze button is an invention of Satan himself. That button is so easy to hit—and causes you to lose your morning a few minutes at a time. Make the decision to simply wake up and get out of bed. Never snooze.

3. *Drink at least sixteen ounces of water as soon as you wake up.* Everyone is dehydrated when they wake up, and that dehydration can lead to hunger, thirst, and foggy thinking. Two cups of water will help stave off hunger until breakfast and make you far more clear-headed than you would otherwise be.

4. *Plan to eat a healthy breakfast.* I (Nelson) go into more detail about the importance of good nutrition in my book *The Healthy Renegade Pastor.* But here, just let me stress that a light, healthy breakfast is a great reward for waking up early. And it gives you an energy boost for the rest of your day.

5. *Reward yourself in other ways for getting up early.* One of the best ways to reward yourself is to schedule some

moderate exercise early in the morning. You will feel better and be healthier when you make exercise a part of your morning routine. Just twenty minutes of physical movement will help you get off to a good start.

6. *Make your bed (or at least your side of the bed if you don't sleep alone).* Making your bed is a signal to your body and mind that sleep time is over and your active day has begun. Studies show that people who make their bed first thing in the morning are more productive overall.

7. *Set a consistent bedtime.* Go to bed at the same time every night. Make sure that your evening obligations end early enough that you can wind down and sleep well. You may have to eliminate or reschedule some evening activities to add an hour to the beginning of your day.

8. *Change the way you think about getting up early.* Instead of lamenting the fact that you *have to* get up early, think of how fortunate you are to *have the privilege* of waking up early. It's a simple change of perspective, but it can help you focus on all there is to gain from waking up early.

9. *Have a plan in place for your morning.* It will be easier to get going if you have a good idea the night before of where you will be going and what you'll be doing. Plan the next day before you go to bed. Then anticipate how great it is going to feel to get a jump on the day.

Admittedly, waking up an hour earlier can be a big adjustment. But a renegade pastor always looks at the rewards inherent in facing and overcoming challenges—and getting up earlier will bring many rewards. So don't wait to begin this important habit. Set that alarm earlier tomorrow, and get up as soon as you hear it!

Chapter 9

TIME ROUTINE ACTIVITIES

How long does it take you to get dressed in the morning? How about to brush your teeth and comb your hair? How much time does it take you to make and eat breakfast? How long does it take to shop for groceries? To go through your mail? To take care of your most frequent household chores? You may have a general idea, but do you really know?

Most of your life is made up of routine tasks. They may not be glamorous or vitally important, but they are necessary. As a renegade pastor, you should know how long these routine activities take, so that you can see where there may be room for time-saving improvement.

Most people don't have a firm idea of the amount of time it takes to do basic things. They estimate and usually end up thinking they can do something more quickly than they actually can. As a result schedules are thrown off. For example, if you think you can get dressed in ten minutes, but it actually takes you fifteen, you will always start your day five minutes behind schedule. And that can snowball until you are late for everything.

Since time is such a precious commodity, you must be intentional about how you are using it. Getting a handle on how long it takes to accomplish the routine things you do every day will be worth the effort. Start by timing each routine task and noting the result. Here's why:

- *You'll discover how much time daily activities really take.* Guessing can get you in trouble in this area. Since routine tasks account for so much of your day, it's important to know exactly how many minutes to allot for them.

- *You'll pinpoint areas in which you can do things more efficiently.* Remember that efficiency involves getting things done more quickly. As you become more aware of how long certain tasks take, you may find new ways to do them just as well in less time.

- *You may realize that you are expending time and effort on some things you don't need to do at all.* As you time yourself, look for activities that are part of your routine but are simply unnecessary. This alone can save you time that can be put toward something more important.

Once you have a handle on how long it takes to get through your routine activities, you can start making the changes necessary to do them more efficiently. It may be a little difficult to change small habits you've had in place for years, but you are a renegade pastor; you aren't afraid of hard work—especially if it means you'll have more time available for fruitful ministry.

RETHINKING YOUR ROUTINE

A routine task is anything you do on a regular basis that you normally do the same way each time. In addition to those mentioned above, the list could include activities like checking your email, going to the dry cleaners, eating meals, getting ready for bed, and the like. Here are five tips to get you started on being more efficient in your routine tasks, whatever they may be:

1. *Focus on one thing at a time.* Effective multitasking is a myth. When you try to multitask you typically end up getting less done overall than when you concentrate on one activity at a time. And what you do accomplish is not as good as it could have been because your full attention isn't on it. Do one routine task at a time. You will do it better and faster.

2. *Plan ahead.* Lay out your clothes the night before. Set out everything where you can easily find it when you need it. You can shave off several minutes every day just by making sure everything you will need is in its place, ready and waiting for you.

3. *Time your down time.* How much time are you really spending on social media (as opposed to how much time you think you're spending)? Be honest about the amount of time you may be whittling away in various ways. The numbers you see on the timer may surprise you.

4. *Think about what you can delegate.* Some of the routine tasks you are currently doing could be done effectively by someone else—which usually means that they should be. (For Nelson's resource on delegation, visit ChurchLeaderInsights.com. Also see Chapter 23: Be Willing to Delegate.)

5. *Give new routines time to become familiar.* Even when you realize that there is a better, more efficient way to do something, you may not see immediate results from changes to your routine. Why? Because it takes time for new habits to form. When you identify something you can do better and make a change, give the new approach at least a month to see how well it will work for you.

A SIMPLE KEY TO GREATER EFFICIENCY

Small changes can result in a lot of time saved. Look at it this way: if you shave one minute a day from your daily routines (a very modest estimate), that alone will save you more than six hours over the course of a year. That's almost a full workday. This little tweak can yield big results. Get out that timer and get started.

Chapter 10

DEVELOP A TEN-MINUTES-EARLY HABIT

Do you know people who are always late? Are you one of them? I (Richard) continually deal with people showing up late for appointments and meetings. Invariably, the person who is late looks harried and offers the pat excuse, "Sorry I'm late. I got stuck in traffic!"

Granted, I live in the Los Angeles area of Southern California. There is always traffic. The freeways and streets are packed at all hours of the day and night. Traffic tie-ups are a normal fact of life here, and they can cause big problems. But often I think the traffic excuse is masking a greater time management problem: most people plan to arrive somewhere on time rather than ten minutes early.

DON'T BE ON TIME—BE EARLY

People arrive late for meetings and appointments every day, all over the world—and they are late because their goal was to be on time. As a renegade pastor, being on time is not the best option; you should always plan on being ten minutes early. Adopting this practice will ensure that you are never late for a meeting again.

Being early for meetings and appointments is more important than most pastors realize. While this may seem to be a minor issue, failing to be punctual reflects very negatively on you. When you're late it tells people that:

- *You are disorganized.* You have trouble juggling all the things you need to do. This is often a consequence of having an overfilled calendar. Disorganized people also tend to either forget to put items on their calendar or to check their calendar on a regular basis.

- *You don't value other people's time.* Being late doesn't just affect your life. It has a domino effect, affecting the time and schedule of everyone else involved in your meeting. When you are late you make everyone else late also. Those people are just as important and busy as you are. Being early shows that you care about them.

- *You don't value your own time.* Again, time is the most valuable resource God gives any of us. When you are late, you are telling people that this precious resource doesn't mean that much to you. Being early shows that you are a good steward of the gift of time God has given you.

- *You are not aware of your surroundings.* There will always be traffic. There will always be lines. There will always be transit delays. You should factor in these things when you are planning how long it will take you to get wherever it is you want to go.

- *You are not reliable.* When you are chronically late the subtle message is that you are less than dependable. Reliability and consistency are vital characteristics people look for in their leaders. When you make it a point to arrive early, you are sending the signal that you are a stable, reliable person who can be trusted.

A SIGN OF DEPENDABILITY AND STRENGTH

Leaders who are consistently late are viewed as weaker and less effective. So being on time should be the standard for every renegade pastor. But we would encourage you to take it a step further and make it your practice to be ten minutes early everywhere you go. Why is this so important?

- *Margin.* Again, making it your goal to be ten minutes early gives you a cushion in case something unforeseen happens. There may be an accident blocking your exit. There may be a line to check in to the building. Any number of scenarios could pop up. Planning to be early ensures that even when something unexpected happens, the chances are you won't be late.

- *Focus.* Getting to a meeting or appointment early gives you time to collect yourself before things get underway. We see it all the time: someone comes running in just as a meeting starts. Then they spend the first ten minutes of the meeting trying to recover from the stress of getting there. They are physically present, but emotionally they're still in a harried rush. Being early gives you a chance to relax and make sure you are mentally present.

- *Minor tasks.* Being early gives you an opportunity to catch up on small tasks that need to be done. That ten minutes of cushion time before a meeting can be a good time to shoot off a quick email response or read an article you've been meaning to get to. It's a good idea to use every small block of time you have available, and being early provides you with an extra one.

- *Networking.* Being early gives you an opportunity to talk to other people who are also there early. You can make some important connections in those few minutes.

Getting places early has a lot of benefits, not the least of which is making you look as though you are in control of your life and your time—which, as a renegade pastor, you are!

HOW TO DEVELOP A TEN-MINUTES-EARLY HABIT

Adopting this habit is surprisingly easy. With some simple changes to your behavior and attitude you can become someone who is consistently early. Here are four practical tips to help you get started:

1. *Change your thinking.* From now on, on time is late and ten minutes early is on time. It's a subtle mental shift that will change the way you approach your schedule.

2. *Allow extra time for travel.* Expect delays and plan accordingly.

3. *Be realistic about how much time you need to prepare.* Many of us think we can get ready for an appointment more quickly than we actually can. Be a realist when you plan.

4. *Avoid back-to-back meetings, if possible.* The second of two consecutive meetings often gets short-changed because the first one ran long. If you must schedule back-to-back, do all you can to wrap up the initial meeting a little early.

For many, being late is a habit. Some even consider it a badge of honor—proof of how busy or important they are. Renegade pastors don't fall into this trap. They demonstrate their mastery of time by making it a point to arrive ten minutes early for everything.

START YOUR DAY TEN MINUTES EARLIER

This habit applies not only to your meetings and appointments with others but also to your commitments to yourself. Applying this principle to getting to work will help you start your day off right. When you work for someone else, you know you have to be at work on time. If you aren't there when you're supposed to be, there may well be consequences. You could lose pay or even your job.

But things are a little different when you pastor a church. For one, instead of working for someone else, other people are now working for you. Or you may be the only person on your staff. Both scenarios make it easy to fall into the bad habit of arriving at the office late. But renegade pastors know this is a big mistake. One of the keys to effectively managing your time is to always be at work when you are expected to be there.

Renegade pastors make it a point to be at work on time every day. There may be no financial consequences for being late, but you will still pay a heavy price. These are just some of the negative ramifications of being late to start your day:

- *You cut into the number of hours you have available to do your job.* This is obvious, but important. There are never enough hours in a day, week, month, or year. When you arrive late, you cut into the fleeting time you are given to do God's work.

- *You rob God.* This may sound harsh, but we believe it's accurate. Pastors have the most important job in the world. Every minute you and I are late is a minute we are taking away from the work God has called us to. We must use our time well in service to our King.

- *You rob your family.* When you show up at the office late, the natural tendency is to stay late. But staying late robs your family of their time with you.

- *You get a bad reputation.* When you have posted office hours (and every pastor should do so), people expect you to be available during those time blocks. If you aren't where you're supposed to be when you're supposed to be there, people see you as unreliable and unable to manage your time. Don't give them reason to come to this conclusion.

- *You set a bad example.* People need to know that you take your vocation seriously, because Kingdom work is serious business. Let them see your example, so they will take seriously the mission to which God has called them.

The simple act of getting to work on time (read: ten-minutes early) will have positive effects for you, your family, and your congregation. In fact, we would argue that committing to being in your office when you are expected to be there is an act of worship, demonstrating that you are serious about devoting your best efforts to the service of God. So, change your thinking, plan ahead, allow yourself some extra travel time and get to your desk on time.

Chapter 11

KEEP ONE CALENDAR

I (Nelson) have the privilege of coaching pastors from all over the world to become better, more effective leaders. Recently one of the members of my Advanced Coaching Network failed to show up for one of our coaching events, which was being held in Florida. When I spoke to him later he confessed that, although he had noted the event on his church's calendar, he had forgotten to add it to his personal calendar.

He didn't remember that he was supposed to be at the coaching event until his wife saw him sitting at the kitchen table on the morning of the event and exclaimed, "I thought you were supposed to be in Orlando!" He was extremely embarrassed—not to mention regretful to have missed out on a great event. This guy is a smart, capable pastor, but he got caught up in the common trap of relying on more than one calendar.

THE POWER OF ONE CALENDAR

Pastors are an extremely busy breed. We have a dozen or more things vying for our attention at any given time. There is no way that any pastor, no matter how intelligent or capable, can possibly keep mental track of everything he needs to do. Add family and church events to the mix, and it becomes impossible to operate well without maintaining a single calendar where you can see at a glance at any time everything that is going on or coming up. There are many benefits to keeping a single written or digital calendar. Here are a few:

- *Keeping a calendar allows you to see at a glance what's going on in your life.* You can take a look at any upcoming day to know what's going to be happening and make note of what time slots you still have free.

- *When you keep a calendar you can make plans as far in advance as necessary.* If you have a kids' choir concert scheduled for two months out, you can go ahead and put it on the calendar. Otherwise it can be all too easy to forget events that are happening well into the future.

- *Calendars are portable.* Whether it is in paper format or on your phone, you can take your calendar with you anywhere—and we suggest that you do. This means that you can immediately note something when it comes up, without having to wait until you get home or to the office to write it down. The longer you wait to make note of an event or commitment, the more likely you are to forget all about it.

- *Setting calendar reminders can help keep you on track.* If you keep your calendar on your phone, or in another digital format, you can set helpful reminders for upcoming events. Setting reminders is a great way to make sure nothing falls through the cracks.

When you don't have a central place to note all of your commitments and activities, you run the risk of missing important events, both in your personal and in your professional life. Nothing makes you look more disorganized (not to mention unreliable and even flaky) than failing to show up for an appointment. Even when you find it necessary to back out at the last minute because of a scheduling conflict, you are broadcasting to the world that you are less than dependable. If you have said you are going to be somewhere, you need to make sure you are there.

MAKING YOUR CALENDAR WORK FOR YOU

The great news is that it is easier today than ever before to keep a single calendar that covers every aspect of your life. You don't even have to be technologically savvy to make this happen. Here are a few tips for making your calendar work for you:

- *Enter everything in your calendar right away.* If you delay, you will forget.

- *Check your calendar daily.* Before you go to bed at night review the day, week, and month ahead so you won't miss anything.

- *Set reminders if you use a digital calendar.* Those reminders are just one more way to make sure you stay on track.

- *Make sure you schedule the important recurring personal events of your life.* Be sure to reserve your daily quiet time, your weekly Sabbath, your date night with your spouse, and your annual vacations.

Just think, with one calendar you will never again have to miss out on an event because you were committed during the same time slot to something else. This makes you look like a leader who has things under control.

You won't schedule church-related appointments on top of planned family events. That shows your family that they are a priority for you. Plus, you will be able to keep your family life and your church life separate, because you will know where you are supposed to be at any given time —and be able to be there without worrying about what you may be missing somewhere else.

So again, to manage your time the renegade way, begin using one calendar to keep track of everything you are involved in, whether personal or professional. You will spare yourself confusion and embarrassment and increase your confidence and focus.

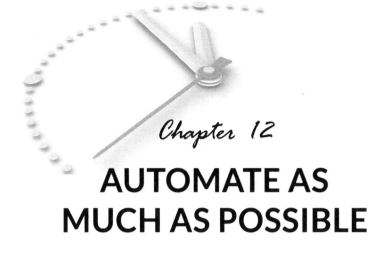

Chapter 12

AUTOMATE AS MUCH AS POSSIBLE

I (Richard) hate bills. Utility bills, credit card bills, all kinds of bills. Actually, what I hate is paying bills. I've always hated writing checks and licking envelopes. As though paying money to utility providers wasn't painful enough, I used to spend an hour or more of my time getting the bills ready to mail. Then came the fun part—a trip to the post office.

But I don't do that anymore. I pay all of my bills online. Instead of spending an hour or more paying bills, I now spend just a few minutes on my phone or laptop. And everything gets paid, with no mistakes.

AMAZING AUTOMATION

We live in amazing times. Technology has made possible conveniences that would have been unthinkable only a few years ago. Renegade pastors need to be on top of technology—not for the sake of having the newest gadgets but because of what technology can do for us. For one, it can save us a lot of time, energy, and stress by helping us automate nearly all the routine activities of our lives.

Too many pastors are reluctant to make use of technology, for a variety of reasons. For some, the idea of doing anything in a new way can seem daunting. Others don't like the idea of ceding control of routine activities to an online service. But let us encourage you to take a step toward automation, even if you've never automated anything before. You'll be able to use the time automation saves you to do more toward fulfilling God's ultimate purpose for you.

WHY YOU SHOULD AUTOMATE

Some people may object that it takes too much work to automate. After all, you will need to educate yourself on automation services. You will have to enter all of your information and preferences before automation can begin. But for renegade pastors automation isn't a luxury—it's a necessity. The benefits of automation far outweigh the initial effort it takes to set up the system. When you automate:

- *You save time every month.* The hours you save will really add up, giving you more time for ministry and family.

- *You save aggravation.* Writing checks, mailing bills, and engaging in other mindless routines can be a time-consuming annoyance. Automation eliminates that aggravation.

- *You save the embarrassment of forgetting something.* In the past, I (Richard) have forgotten to mail a utility payment, only to receive in the mail a bright red bill with the words DISCONNECTION NOTICE prominently displayed on the envelope. If I had automated that wouldn't have happened.

WHAT YOU CAN AUTOMATE

Many routine activities can be automated. Here are just a few:

- *Bill Pay*: Utility bills, mortgage payments, credit card invoices, phone bills, cable bills, etc. Just about any bill that comes to you on a regular basis can be automated. Even if your bank or the respective company charges a small fee to automate, the amount of time and stress you save are worth it.

- *Computer Backup:* You can sign up for a service that automatically backs up your computer files online. All computers eventually die. If you haven't properly backed up everything—a confusing, time-consuming process for most people—you will lose all your files. Automation can pay off big time in this area.

- *Groceries:* In many cities you can arrange to have your groceries delivered, saving you the time it takes to go to the store and shop. You can create a list of the items you purchase regularly, shop from that list online when you need something, and the groceries will be delivered right to your door.

- *Planned Meals:* In many families, meal planning is a major time-consumer. There are many services that will send you weekly meal plans and recipes (and sometimes even deliver the ingredients). All you have to do is cook and enjoy!

There is virtually no limit to what you can automate in your home, from programming your thermostat to locking or unlocking your door to monitoring home security. You can control all of this from apps on your phone. And as technology moves forward there will be even more things that can be automated. Keep abreast of new developments as they come out and you will find more ways to save time and avoid aggravation.

REMINDERS TO OPTIMIZE AUTOMATION

Automation can be a tremendous benefit for every renegade pastor. But there are a few things you need to keep in mind to optimize your experience:

- *Keep an eye on your services.* I (Richard) had an unpleasant experience recently. I received a call from my insurance agent. Our auto insurance, which is paid automatically, was being cancelled due to lack of payment. Apparently my credit union had for whatever reason stopped sending the payment I had set up. I should have been keeping a better eye on things.

- *Be mindful of security.* Use only banks and services that have good track records regarding security. It's a dangerous world out there, with people constantly trying to steal your personal information. Make sure you use strong passwords for your accounts and change them often.

With these warnings in place, you should be able to enjoy automation and its benefits. As a renegade pastor you will benefit from taking advantage of this key to good time management.

Chapter 13

PLAN YOUR DAY BEFORE YOU START YOUR DAY

Pastor Joe Average prides himself on being flexible. He likes to say that he lets God plan his day. When he gets to his office, often a bit late, he jumps into whatever project or meeting seems to be the most urgent. Although his flexibility might be something of a virtue on one level, it causes him great frustration in many areas. People who don't make enough noise usually can't get his attention. His sermon preparation suffers regularly. And he doesn't maintain set office hours, so people often have a hard time pinning him down when they need something.

Renegade pastors can't afford to operate in this way. We understand that if you don't plan your day and stick to that plan, you will spend the day pulled in the direction of every urgent (but not necessarily important—see Chapter 4) claim for your attention that pops up. Your day will be filled with things that may not be the best use of your time—things you may not even need, let alone want, to do. Renegade pastors are intentional about planning their day before it starts.

DAILY PLANNING DOS

To be effective as a leader you must adopt the practice of scheduling your day before it begins. It's just that simple—and this is one of the best approaches to managing your time well. Planning each day will take just a few minutes but will make you exponentially more productive.

How do renegade pastors plan ahead (whether they do so every morning or even the night before)? Here are a few tips for scheduling your day for maximum effectiveness:

- *Plan according to your values.* Make sure you spend time every day in Quadrant 2 (see Chapter 4), the quadrant in which you invest time in what's most important rather than what's most urgent. Those are the things that will lead not only to increased effectiveness, but also to more peace and satisfaction.

- *Be realistic about how much time you will need to complete every task.* Many pastors think they can do things faster than they actually can. That leads to being constantly behind schedule. Renegade pastors are realistic about what they are able to do and plan accordingly.

- *Plan specific times for checking email.* It is easy to become a slave to your inbox, checking your email every few minutes. Instead, designate a specific time or times throughout the day when you will check and answer email. You can let people know that they should not expect an immediate response from you, even though you are diligent to respond promptly.

- *Plan your devotional time.* What you don't schedule often doesn't get done. So be sure to schedule your time alone with God. It may not seem very spiritual to put this on your calendar, but what better way to show that you are serious about spending time with your heavenly Father than to make a daily appointment and stick with it?

- *Schedule according to your body's natural circadian rhythms.* Some people have more energy and a clearer head early in the morning, while others don't feel human until after lunch. Whenever possible, work with the way you are wired. Plan your most important and most taxing activities for the time periods when you are more likely to be at your best. Plan more menial tasks for time blocks when you are likely to have less energy to give.

- *Set deadlines.* Nearly everything you do should have a deadline for completion. That includes meetings, sermon preparation, and most other matters that come across your desk. Deadlines act as catalysts for accomplishment. When you don't set them, tasks tend to drag on longer than they should. (See Chapter 15: Set Deadlines.)

- *Plan your daily exit.* Your family is even more important than your work as pastor. Plan when you are going to go home—and stick to the plan. Don't rob your family of precious, important time with you by staying at the office too late.

- *Plan blocks of personal time.* People are our most important priority. But they can also be tremendous time-wasters. Average pastors have an open-door policy for anyone who wants to drop in and talk. Renegade pastors have scheduled times when they are available and other times when they are not. Plan and use blocks of personal time for your most intense work, for things that demand your complete concentration.

When you plan according to these guidelines, you will be more productive. You will also experience greater peace of mind because you will know what you are supposed to be doing at any given moment and have a good idea of what's coming next.

DAILY PLANNING DON'TS

Planning your day ahead of time will save enormous amounts of time and stress. But there are a few things to be aware of in your planning that can sidetrack you. Keep these planning don'ts:

- *Don't neglect to plan daily.* You must develop the discipline of planning every day. Otherwise you'll miss out on the full benefits of planning. When you fail to plan each day things can begin to snowball. Before you know it, you'll find yourself a week behind in several areas simply because you skipped a day or two of proper planning.

- *Don't forget to balance people time against project time.* It's easy to plan tasks and ignore people. Or you can err in the opposite direction, spending time with people at the expense of important tasks. Renegade pastors learn to balance public and private time.

- *Don't be late.* Chapter 10 details the importance of arriving everywhere ten minutes early. That includes arriving at work ten minutes early. Again, it may be easy to fudge on your work hours and get to your office a little (or a lot) late. Don't fall into this trap. You will accomplish more if you start your day on time. Plus, the discipline of arriving early each day is valuable in and of itself.

- *Don't forget to plan prayerfully.* Planning is a spiritual exercise, an act of faith. Make sure to regularly pray the Time Management Prayer: "What is the best use of my time right now?" (See Chapter 5.) Trust God to answer this prayer. He will give you wisdom about how to plan your day.

Plan your day before it starts. This is an easy and effective way to save time, experience greater peace and confidence, and become a better leader. It also helps you devote more time to your family—time when you can be focused on them and not on church commitments. This is something you can start right away. Take the time right now to plan the rest of your day and your tomorrow.

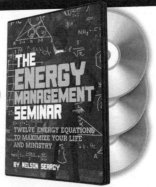

Chapter 14

MAKE A TOP SIX LIST

I (Richard) struggled for a long time to consistently make and follow through on to-do lists. Once, I signed up for an online service that would help me keep track of my to-do list. This service would email me a copy of my list every morning so I would have it when I got to work. If I hadn't created a new list the night before, the system would automatically carry over my list from previous days.

The trouble was that I would often go for weeks without opening those emails. When I would open them I always saw tasks I had completed weeks earlier. Sometimes I would see tasks I had forgotten about or decided not to pursue. This service, although it provided everything I needed, was useless to me simply because I didn't commit to using it.

Over the years I have come to see the error of my ways, and the incredible benefit of keeping an active, updated to-do list. I now keep such a list, which helps me stay on track with the many things I need to do during the day. Keeping a to-do list is essential for renegade pastors who want to be proactive about spending their time on things that matter.

THE DIFFICULTY IN A TO-DO LIST

A to-do list is a powerful time management tool. It will clarify and simplify your life. It will save you the time you may be wasting during the day trying to figure out what to do next. Still, many people find it difficult to make and keep an effective to-do list. There are several factors that play in to the common to-do list struggle, including:

- *No list at all.* No matter how great your list-making skills are, they won't matter unless you make a list. This is one of the many areas of life in which a small investment of time will reap huge time savings every day. So take a few minutes to jot down a list. The result will be well worth the effort.

- *Not checking the list regularly.* Writing out a great list that you never look at is a waste of time and energy. You must check your list regularly to keep yourself on track.

- *Having too many large items on the list.* Most pastors are big-picture thinkers. They see the scope of a project that needs to be done but sometimes underestimate the details necessary to making it happen. To-do lists are the place to log and track the small items that go into accomplishing big things.

- *Failure to prioritize.* Not everything you do is of equal importance. Your to-do list should be prioritized to highlight what's most important; we'll discuss this a little later.

- *Not having the list in a convenient, accessible location.* Be certain that your list is in a place where you can look at it several times throughout the day. The most convenient place to keep a to-do list may be on your phone, since it's usually handy.

YOUR TOP SIX LIST

While we don't have the space here to offer a full treatise on to-do lists, we can help you with a few ideas to make your list much more effective. One factor that will help tremendously is to limit the size of your list. Let's face it: a pastor never has a shortage of tasks to accomplish. There are always activities, meetings, sermon and worship prep, and a dozen other things competing for our attention.

Your to-do list should reflect the most important things you need to accomplish. Every day there will be any number of good things you'll have to let go to get the most important tasks accomplished. Having too many to-dos on your list can cause stress and keep you from focusing as you should on the task at hand. That's why we suggest limiting your to-do list to six items per day. Beyond that you are probably trying to accomplish too much, which will do nothing but sabotage your effectiveness.

Renegade pastors don't just make to-do lists; they make to-do lists that work. Keep these keys in mind when putting together your list:

- *Make your list the night before.* Writing out your list the night before frees you up to begin working as soon as you get to the office. Plus, when you make the list the night before your subconscious goes to work on it—finding solutions to problems and planning the best way to get things done—while you sleep.

- *Put only the six most important items on your list.* Leave off the minor things. Focus on the activities that will have the greatest impact on your life and ministry. Ask yourself two questions to decide whether something should be on your list:
  1. Does it need to be done?
  2. Can someone else do it?

If it is something that should be done and can't be delegated, put it on your list.

- *Estimate how much time it will take to accomplish each task.* Set a realistic timetable for every item. You don't want to schedule fourteen hours' worth of work, for example, for your ten-hour work day.

- *Use active words as you write your list.* What, specifically, do you intend to accomplish with regard to each task? Spell it out in colorful, active language. This will help motivate you to tackle the job and will encourage you to think in terms of the action steps that will need to happen.

- *Break large projects into smaller, specific tasks.* It is easy to get overwhelmed by the big projects we need to do, especially when they may take days or weeks to complete. Break those projects into manageable chunks that can be achieved in more confined time periods. Then add those steps to your list.

Every renegade pastor should keep a to-do list that is concise and priority-driven. It will save you time energy and a lot of frustration. And you can start using one right away. Take a few minutes tonight to make your Top Six List for tomorrow. In the morning you will be very happy you did.

Chapter 15

SET DEADLINES

Have you ever noticed that you are able to accomplish more the day before you leave for a vacation than any other day? You may have a stack of things to do, but knowing that you can't leave anything undone, you manage to get to it all.

Why does this happen? Simply because you know there's no alternative. There is a firm deadline. You must finish your work before you go, so you find a way to get it done. The good news is that you can put this principle to work for yourself any time, not just when you are going on vacation. Setting deadlines will always help you get more done more quickly.

THE MAGIC OF DEADLINES

You should attach a deadline to every task you need to accomplish. This is a simple, practical step that will help you get exponentially more done every day. Here are several key reasons to start setting deadlines:

- *Deadlines help you focus.* When there's an end time set, you tend to work diligently on one task. You don't have time to split your attention by multitasking. Knowing that you must be done at a certain time keeps a project moving forward.

- *Deadlines help you prioritize.* Time is a finite resource, so it's important to prioritize wisely. Deadlines can help keep you engaged with the things that really matter. Schedule your most important projects first; then you can give any additional time to tasks that are not quite as important.

- *Deadlines help you get other people involved.* Most of your church volunteers—and staff, for that matter—lack time or energy to devote to never-ending tasks. When you set deadlines you can ask for commitments that will require a specified amount of time. People are much more likely to say yes to projects that have a defined time commitment attached to them.

- *Deadlines motivate you.* Deadlines provide the push you may need to get a project done. There are consequences associated with missing a deadline that no one wants to experience. We would much rather reap the reward of having completed a task when we said we were going to complete it.

- *Deadlines provide momentum.* Think of deadlines met as wins, both for you personally and for your church. The more you win, the more winning will become a habit. Every win—every accomplished task—you momentum to do it again and again.

SEVEN KEYS TO SETTING EFFECTIVE DEADLINES

Deadlines are an important tool. Try to attach one to every task you add to your to-do list. Keep the following seven keys in mind to help you start setting deadlines like a pro:

1. *Decide whether the proposed task is worth doing.* As mentioned previously, don't waste your time on activities that either don't need to be done or could be performed by someone else. Prioritizing is vital.

2. *Be realistic.* It is easy to be overly optimistic when setting deadlines. Make a realistic assessment of what it will take to get something done, and then schedule your deadline accordingly. Otherwise, you will be setting yourself up for failure and frustration.

3. *Be specific.* Clear deadlines are easier to meet than foggy ones. Make sure you are as specific as possible with each one. For example, setting a deadline like "Finish a chunk of *The Renegade Pastor's Guide to Time Management* book by 5 p.m." is okay, but "Finish twelve hundred words by 5 p.m." is more specific and quantifiable and thus far more preferable.

4. *Break large projects into manageable parts.* If a project deadline is too far in the future, or the project is too large to get a handle on, it can be hard to motivate yourself to get started. A better plan is to focus on smaller parts of the large task and set deadlines for each of those. As you check off the smaller tasks, the larger one will "magically" get completed.

5. *Reward yourself for meeting deadlines.* Again, there are consequences for not getting things done in a timely manner. There should also be rewards for finishing tasks on time. When you meet a big deadline, schedule an extra hour of reading or take your spouse out for a date night. Such intentional rewards provide powerful motivation for getting things done.

6. *Don't be afraid to ask for help.* You and I can always get further faster when we work together. Solicit others to join your team to help accomplish what needs to get done. You will get more done, and you will give others the satisfaction of being part of working in God's Kingdom.

7. *Let others hold you accountable.* Have someone else—a staff member, another church member or pastor—know what your deadlines are, and give that person permission to check in with you. Knowing that you are being held accountable will keep you going when you may feel like stopping.

Deadlines are key to accomplishing more tasks, more effectively, every day. Learn to use them often and well in your journey toward renegade time management.

Chapter 16

FIND FOCUS

Pastor Joe Average is busy all the time. He starts his day working on his message for the weekend. Soon emails start coming in. He has to see what they are—and the important ones need to be answered. He also has to keep tabs on the church's social media outlets, so he checks each one a few times during the course of the day. He gets phone calls from church members and from his family and tries to make time for everyone.

The result? Pastor Joe rarely gets as much done in a day as he has planned. He sets deadlines for each task he tackles but consistently misses them. Feeling himself pulled in an infinite number of directions, he feels as though he can't ever give his full attention to any one project.

Rob Renegade's day looks entirely different. He also sets deadlines for the things on his to-do list, and he almost always meets those targets. When working, he focuses on the task at hand, without the distractions of phone calls or the intrusion of social media. In fact, he turns off all his notifications and mutes the ringer on his phone while he is engaged in something important. He keeps track of social media but checks it at designated times of the day—and then only for a moment. He returns phone calls faithfully, but at the specified times he has set aside.

One of the biggest differences between Pastor Joe and Pastor Rob comes down to a single word: *focus*. Pastor Rob works within the reality that you can only do one thing at a time well. He is focused on what he needs to do and he does it. He can be trusted. His family gets his full attention when he is with them. He is successful and fruitful in his personal life and ministry. Pastor Joe, on the other hand, gets distracted and off-track easily, leading to ineffectiveness and a multitude of related problems. Focus is key to accomplishing great things for God's Kingdom.

HOW DISTRACTED ARE YOU?

Distraction will come at you in many different forms, including:

- Internet surfing

- Social media activity

- Phone calls

- Emails

- Unplanned meetings

- A belief in multitasking

- Online movies and television shows

- Reading (when we should be doing something else)

If you aren't careful, these things and others have the potential to sabotage your day. You must be intentional about finding focus—about concentrating on a single task for an allotted time or, as we like to say, working all the time you work. Focus is key to renegade time management.

FIVE WAYS TO FIND FOCUS

Use these five tips to help you work with focus and effectiveness all the time you're working:

1. *Set a specific time for checking social media.* Social media is an important part of our lives, but it can also be a huge time-waster. Instead of checking it throughout the day, schedule a small block of time to check your church and personal accounts. At all other times log out of your accounts and turn off phone notifications. That will remove the temptation to hop on "for just a minute." Those minutes can easily turn into an hour or more.

2. *Schedule a time to respond to email and phone calls.* I (Richard) turn off my ringer when I'm working, so I don't hear people calling or texting me. But I have specific times when I check my phone and email, and I respond promptly. I find that I get more done, and people know I'm going to get back to them as soon as possible.

3. *Schedule according to your energy levels.* If you're a morning person, schedule your most taxing tasks for the mornings. Better after lunch? Then that's when you should tackle the tasks that require the most focus.

4. *Spend as much time as possible working in areas you're passionate about.* Those are the areas where you will work with the greatest focus and the most energy.

5. *Treat your brain like the muscle it is.* When you lift weights, the key is to keep increasing the weights bit by bit as you get stronger. Try the same approach with your brain. Start by working in focused ten-minute time

blocks with five-minute breaks. Work your way up to full concentration for fifty minutes, and then take a ten-minute stretch break.

When you commit to finding focus, your productivity will skyrocket. As an added bonus you'll discover that you enjoy your family time and your off time even more when you are working with diligence the whole time you are at work. What you are doing is eternally significant, so do all you can to be fully focused every minute of the day.

Chapter 17

ORGANIZE YOUR DESK

The desk clutter struggle is real for pastors. And it's no surprise. After all, there are few other professions that have more activities going on at the same time. A lot of those activities lead to plans, outlines, memos, receipts, and other items being deposited on your desk. It doesn't take long for it to get out of control. You may have even resigned yourself to the fact that you will always have a cluttered desk. It's just part of the job, right?

THE COST OF A CLUTTERED DESK

Wrong. Average pastors may consider a cluttered desk to be a necessary evil—but not so with renegade pastors. As a renegade you should be more aware of the dangerous effects that can result from a cluttered desk. A cluttered desk means that:

- *You will eventually lose or forget something.* You may think you know what's buried in each pile of paperwork on your desk, but you probably don't. Eventually something important will fall through the cracks because you forgot it was waiting at the bottom of a desk pile.

- *You will lose time looking for things.* Time spent searching for something on your desk is time wasted. Even if you save only a few minutes every week by keeping your desk organized, you will gain several hours per year for fruitful ministry.

- *You will get frustrated.* Spending valuable time searching for things, coupled with the pain of forgetting something, will inevitably increase your frustration level—and no pastor needs added frustration.

- *You won't be able to focus as well on the important things.* A messy desk leads to mental clutter. The more mental clutter you have, the less you are able to focus on the important things you need to do.

In addition, a cluttered desk (and clutter in general) decreases your enthusiasm and your peace of mind. For all of these reasons and more, it is important that you get your desk under control.

KEYS TO AN ORGANIZED DESK

Keeping your desk clean is an ongoing job. You can't just organize it once and expect it to stay that way. But every minute you spend organizing your desk will result in ten minutes of increased productivity. Taking a little time regularly to clean up and organize will be well worth the effort.

So how can you go about doing this ? Are there some ways of organizing your desk that are more effective than others? Yes! Here are seven keys to getting your desk under control:

1. *Start by clearing everything off your desk.* Everything. Throw away obvious trash. It's time to start over from the beginning. You don't have to put anything back the way it was. This is a new, more productive, more efficient day.

2. *Throw away everything old and outdated.* Do you really need that funny desk calendar from three years ago? Probably not. And Christmas cards should be nowhere to be seen, unless you happen to be doing this in the month of December. Throw away obsolete items, and store or file anything with purely sentimental value.

3. *Keep your most essential items closest to you.* When you are putting your desk back together, think in terms of efficiency. If you use note paper a lot, place a pad where you can reach it easily. The same is true of paper clips and other items you use often. Keep these items within arm's reach. And make sure you have enough supplies on hand to get your work done.

4. *Keep nonessential items that you still use regularly in drawers near you.* We all have certain things we use a lot, but not on a daily or hourly basis. Staplers and writing utensils often fall into this category. Keep them handy in nearby drawers so they are easily reached, but out of the way.

5. *Consider procuring a desk drawer organizer for smaller items.* Paper clips, staples, sticky notes, and pens can easily go into their own little compartments in a desk drawer, where they will be easy to retrieve when you need them.

6. *File paperwork immediately.* Don't let anything sit on your desk if you aren't working on it. If the paperwork is something you will need to come back to later, schedule a time to do so on your calendar and make a note of where you filed whatever paperwork you'll need.

7. *Store anything you aren't using.* Consider discarding materials and supplies from a completed project or something you aren't going to be working with any time soon. If you decide you want to keep them, label them clearly and store them.

And, since keeping your desk organized can be the most difficult part, here is one more tip:

8. *Be intentional about maintaining your new clutter-free space.* Always put things back in their proper place when you're finished with them. File completed paperwork right away. Taking care of the small stuff on an immediate basis will help you keep your desk under control.

The rewards of maintaining an organized desk—among them peace of mind, increased focus, a sense of being on top of everything that's going on around you—all are worth the effort it takes to get there and stay there. For renegade pastors, a clean, organized desk isn't just nice to have—it's a necessity!

Chapter 18

EAT THE FROG

Frogs. They're everywhere. As a matter of fact, I'm sure frogs interrupt your day every day. A frog is a big, ugly task—one you would rather not have to face. So you let it sit there on your desk, staring you down. Occasionally it ribbits, waiting for you to do something. It hops up and down to get your attention. You can always see it just out of the corner of your eye. It's wart-covered and slimy. And it keeps growing. That frog gets bigger and bigger until he makes it hard for you to concentrate on anything else you need to do.

You may want to ignore the frogs in your life, but this never works. Eventually you'll have to deal with them. You can't escape those tasks that are unpleasant but necessary. When you try, certain consequences will happen every time:

- *Your energy will be zapped.* That frog on your desk will suck away your energy, diverting it from every other task you need to accomplish. The other things you need to do will be harder to accomplish because so much of your energy will be taken up by worrying about and gearing up for the unpleasant task you know you need to complete.

- *You will be distracted.* Your thoughts will constantly go back to that frog. You will be so preoccupied, knowing you have to tackle the tough task ahead of you, that your concentration will be pulled from the work you are currently doing.

- *The frog will grow.* Our fears always grow when we refuse to face them head-on. Procrastination makes every unpleasant task worse than it should be. When we delay we lose perspective, and that frog starts to get bigger and bigger.

THE SOLUTION

There is only one solution for dealing with the frogs in your life: *eat them.* Yes, you've read that correctly! What does it mean to eat the frog? Simply this: attack it early. Conquer it. Get that thing done and off your desk, no matter how unpleasant it may be. Then your time and energy will be freed up to handle tasks that are equally important but much more pleasant. Renegade pastors know that eating frogs is never fun, but it's one of the best time management tools that exists.

The thought of eating ugly, slimy frogs is disgusting, right? Handling some of the tasks that ministry throws at you can be truly disgusting. But being proactive and facing them head on is the only answer. Those difficult tasks seldom, if ever, hop away on their own. Too often, in fact, if you leave them undone they'll get worse, until they morph into true crises. When you eat the frog there may be a moment of unpleasantness, but then it's over and you can move on.

HOW TO EAT A FROG

There are certain things you can do to make frog-eating a slightly better experience. You might even find that you come to enjoy tackling unpleasant tasks. Keep these tips in mind:

- *Be honest about which tasks are unpleasant.* You generally know ahead of time if something is going to be particularly difficult. Does it involve difficult people? Is it something you are unskilled or inexperienced in? Will it force you outside your comfort zone? All of these things make an activity a frog. Acknowledge that reality.

- *Eat the frog early.* Don't let it sit on your desk all day, watching your every move. Get rid of it before it grows. Make eating frogs the first thing you do in the morning. Frog meat is the breakfast of champions.

- *Take small bites, if needed.* Sometimes a task becomes a frog simply because it is so big. When you cut it down into smaller pieces, it may not be so daunting.

- *Remember the benefits of eating frogs.* Think about the results of the unpleasant task. Will you get a difficult staff member on board with the vision of the church? Will you achieve greater clarity in a difficult area of ministry? Will a particular church member move from being skeptical about your leadership to becoming a fan? Often, those difficult tasks reap big rewards. Look past the short-term pain to see the long-term benefit.

WHAT EATING FROGS WILL DO FOR YOU

Tackling unpleasant tasks early, before they become disasters, is an essential time management skill. You will find that doing so has a tremendous impact on you personally, as well as on your ministry. Here are a few of the things you can expect when you develop the habit of eating frogs:

- *Your focus will improve.* When you no longer have that nasty task hanging over your head, you will be able to concentrate more fully on the other things you need to do.

- *Your energy will skyrocket.* With improved focus comes enhanced energy. When dread isn't weighing you down, your energy reserves are freed up for other tasks at hand.

- *Your confidence will grow.* The more difficult things you tackle, the more confidence you will have. And the more confidence you have, the better you will be at tackling difficult things.

- *Your faith will grow.* When you face tasks that require you to fully use the gifts and talents God has given you, you'll find that God has equipped you with everything you need to accomplish his purpose for your life.

- *Your reputation as a leader will grow.* When people see that you are willing to face and handle difficult things, they will respect you more. They'll know you can be trusted and followed.

Try to view those frogs that hop into your office as opportunities rather than obstacles. Opportunities to grow. Opportunities to become the person and the pastor God has called you to be. Renegade pastors learn to love eating frogs, because they know that each frog is a stepping stone to greater accomplishment and effectiveness. So don't be afraid of the frogs. Get out your fork and take a bite.

Chapter 19

TOUCH IT ONCE

I (Richard) used to have a terrible habit of letting mail pile up. Because I have automated all my monthly bills, and because most of my friends contact me via text or email, I get very little snail mail that is important. I always knew that I should go through the mail as it came in, but instead I allowed it to pile up by my mail slot. After a few days I would sift through it—and put it back in the same pile, or maybe start another pile that I would promise myself to "go through later." What usually ended up happening was that I became disgusted after several days. Can you relate? Thank goodness I have gotten better about this.

THE AVERAGE WAY OF DEALING WITH ROUTINE TASKS

Average pastors (a description of myself when it came to handling my daily mail) often have a habit of moving things around without completing them. Then they have to go back to those things again and again. If you have adopted this ineffective habit, it's time to kick it. It is making you far less efficient and effective.

When you simply move things around—or touch them repeatedly—the result is mental clutter. The various uncompleted tasks and unopened items drain you of mental energy, resulting in scattered focus, waning enthusiasm, and a diminished ability to tackle the demanding activities on your plate.

The time management technique we refer to as *Touch It Once* will help you get gain control of over the small, seemingly inconsequential tasks that come up every day. Those little things may not be important in themselves, but they can become big time and energy wasters when we allow them to pile up. And there is simply no need for them to become major issues. You have enough things to handle that are truly important. You can't let yourself get bogged down by small things.

BIGGEST AREAS OF STRUGGLE

Most average pastors have at least one area in which they struggle to "touch it once":

- *Physical mail:* Mail is easy to set aside, as you tell yourself you'll tackle it later.

- *Email:* Email can quickly pile up and leave you feeling behind and even panicky. How often have you read an email and thought, "I should respond to this now," only to move on and leave it hanging?

- *Clothes:* The chore of laundry can lead to piles of clothes that are set aside to wash but left untouched, or left in the washer so long they need to be run through the cycle again. Somewhere between the sorting, washing, drying, folding, and putting away, clothes can pile up and begin to feel unmanageable.

- *Cleaning:* When you can't decide where to focus, several random cleaning chores may get partially or halfheartedly completed with the overall job left incomplete.

- *Any number of small tasks:* Mundane tasks tend to be boring, so it's easy to shuffle them around from time to time without truly accomplishing anything. They become part of our mental clutter.

A BETTER WAY TO HANDLE ROUTINE TASKS

If you recognize yourself in any of the above scenarios, you need to learn the Touch It Once technique. It's simple: when you see a small, routine, or mundane task that needs to be done, just do it. Do it in one sitting and get it out of the way.

Touch It Once is a rallying cry that will help you decide how to deal with any task that comes across your desk, whether at work or at home. It provides a boundary for analyzing every job and determining the best course of action. While simple, Touch It Once will take some practice before it becomes a habit. To get started with the technique, make these four decisions for every routine task that comes up:

1. *Decide whether something needs to be done at all and then decide if it needs to be done by you.* Some things will cross your desk that simply don't need to be done—so don't do them. Let them go. And remember that you don't need to do everything yourself. If someone else can handle it, let them. Release control. That will free you to concentrate on the things that only you can do.

2. *Consider if it is a repeated task that can be automated.* If you can automate a task, the effort can save hours of work for years to come. (See Chapter 12: Automate as Much as Possible.)

3. *Decide whether the task can be done in five minutes or less.* If it can, and you are the best one to do it, then just get it done. Don't let little things hang around and become bigger than they need to be.

4. *If a task needs to be done, needs to be done by you, and can't be done in less than five minutes, schedule it on your calendar.* Schedule time for the larger things that are going to take a little more focus and energy.

The Touch It Once technique will help you gain control over those little tasks that come up every day, both in ministry and in life.

Chapter 20

WRITE IT DOWN

Have you ever run into this scenario? A distraught church member comes up to you and tells you about something traumatic going on in her life. You listen attentively, address her concerns, give her godly counsel, and end the conversation with, "I will pray for you!" You then promptly forget to pray—until the next time you see her. You send up some quick make-up prayers and hope you will be better about remembering the next time around.

The reason you forget to pray in this kind of situation isn't a lack of concern or spiritual laziness. It's much more basic: you didn't write down the request. You and I talk to so many different people over the course of a day or week that we can't possibly remember the details of every conversation. That's why it's important to develop the habit of writing things down right away.

CONSEQUENCES OF FORGETFULNESS

You likely rely on your memory far too much. You think you will remember what you hear or things you need to do, but it isn't reasonable to believe that you can or will remember everything. You're busy. You're human. You *will* forget things—even important things. But forgetting what you need to remember can have some very negative consequences. Here are just a few:

- *You will disappoint church and community members.* When people ask you to pray for them, you need to be able to honestly assure them that you have prayed. When you say you are going to do some kind of community ministry and then forget to show up, the people involved will be disappointed.

- *You will disappoint family members.* The first time you forget your child's sporting event or the dinner reservation you made for yourself and your spouse, you will be reminded how important it is to write everything down immediately. Don't let this happen to you.

- *Your church will suffer.* That event you forget, or that person you disappoint because you didn't remember to call them, may be key to the growth and health of your church. This isn't just about you—your entire church may pay the price of your forgetfulness.

- *Your reputation as a leader will suffer.* People look up to you as a role model. They expect you to be reliable and to keep your word. When you forget you send a clear signal that you can't be trusted. People won't follow someone they can't trust.

Any one of these consequences should be enough to spur you to develop the habit of immediately writing down important things. When you put them all together, you can see that this isn't just a good suggestion; it's a necessity for any renegade pastor.

WRITE IT DOWN RIGHT AWAY

Anything that's important, anything you need to do, and anything you want to remember about a person or a conversation needs to be written down. Anything. Everything. And you must do it immediately.

You cannot simply hope you'll remember to write something down later on. Don't put that burden on yourself. Just do it right away— and then put it where you can easily access the information. Making a habit of writing things down immediately will benefit you in many ways. Here are just four ways this practice will improve your life:

1. *Greater peace of mind.* You will no longer have that nagging fear that you may be forgetting something.

2. *Better focus.* When you have less mental clutter, it frees you to concentrate on what you are doing now.

3. *Happier church and family life.* Everyone wins when you are dependable. Be someone the people around you can count on.

4. *Better reputation in the community.* Keep your word, and even people who disagree with you will admit that you are a person of integrity. That goes a long way in our profession.

TWO IMPORTANT WORDS

As you develop the habit of immediately writing down every important item, keep these two key words in mind: *accessibility* and *reminders*.

1. *Accessibility.* Make sure you can easily retrieve the things you write down. Consider getting an app for your phone, preferably one that syncs with your computer, tablet, and other devices. I (Richard) regularly use an app called Good ToDo, which allows me to create to-do lists I can access anywhere. But it really doesn't matter whether you use online calendars and apps or an old-fashioned paper

calendar and to-do list, as long as you make sure you have a system that works for you.

2. *Reminders.* The best system in the world is useless unless you remember to follow through on the information or prompts recorded on it. Try setting reminders to aid your memory. When you see that reminder pop up on your phone, it means it's time to get something done.

DON'T RELY ON YOUR MEMORY

Give your memory a break. It can't possibly handle all that you have going on in your personal life, family life, and ministry. Start writing down everything right away. When you do, you'll increase your productivity, your peace of mind, and your standing as a leader. That's more than worth the few seconds it takes to jot down a note!

Chapter 21

WORK IN BLOCKS OF TIME

When I (Richard) started a church several years ago, I had to take an outside job to make ends meet. Since I was a pretty good writer, I decided to try my hand at writing marketing and promotional materials on a freelance basis. I ended up earning a living for several years as a freelance writer. It was hard work, but I was able to support my family doing it.

One of the most valuable lessons I learned from freelancing was the benefit of the Fifty-Minute Frenzy. This is a term used to describe a specific, focused period of time where you do nothing but write. When that chunk of time is over, you walk away from the computer for a ten or fifteen-minute break. Then you sit down for another Fifty-Minute Frenzy.

I still use this tool today. In fact, it's the approach I take when putting together a sermon. The Fifty-Minute Frenzy works for a few reasons:

1. It has a set end time, which encourages you to work while you can.

2. It has a built-in break to clear and refresh your mind.

3. It focuses your attention on one area of work.

102 THE *Renegade* PASTOR'S GUIDE TO TIME MANAGEMENT

The Fifty-Minute Frenzy is simply an example of time blocking—the time management practice of devoting solid chunks of time to a single task or single type of task. To be most effective you'll need to perform similar tasks at one sitting whenever possible. The opposite approach, in which you jump from one activity to the next with little continuity, kills focus and efficiency.

WORKING IN BLOCKS OF TIME

Pastors wear so many hats—preacher, counselor, human resources manager, maybe even plumber—that it may seem impossible at first to group similar tasks into blocks of time. Many of us are so accustomed to jumping from one activity to another that it would be hard to break the cycle. But for renegade pastors, working in blocks of time is a great tool for increasing work productivity. It maximizes your focus and energy and can dramatically impact the fruitfulness of your ministry. There are several reasons why this approach is so effective:

- *It gives you a starting point.* Have you ever been so overwhelmed with what you need to accomplish that you feel paralyzed? When you block time, you eliminate the feeling of not knowing where to begin. Your time is planned and you know exactly where to start.

- *It eliminates distractions.* Your best work is going to be done when you are least distracted. Time blocking keeps you focused on one thing at a time, which is the best way to work.

- *It helps you complete important tasks more effectively.* The biggest, most important tasks of your ministry require as much concentration as possible. Time blocking inherently concentrates your focus, so you can take care of the important things well.

- *It increases motivation.* If something is important enough for you to block out a chunk of time to complete it, then it must be truly significant. That realization, along with the commitment you made by blocking out the time, naturally increases your motivation to get it done.

- *It can help you say no more easily.* Many pastors have difficulty saying no to people. We want to agree to be a part of every worthwhile activity that comes along. But when you have scheduled blocks of time already committed to other projects, saying no gets easier. You can honestly say, "I'd love to do that, but I have another commitment."

FIVE KEYS FOR EFFECTIVE TIME BLOCKING

For many renegade pastors, working in time blocks is a new skill. But, with some simple planning, you can get started right away. Here are five keys for using time blocking effectively:

1. *Put your blocks on your schedule and then guard them zealously.* Work everything else in your schedule around your time blocks. Don't let other activities or distractions encroach on what you need to do during those times. After all, what you will accomplish during your time blocks is essential to the success of your life and ministry.

2. *Create time blocks for your highest-priority activities.* Not everything you do is worth the reservation of a time block. Reserve blocks for the things that will have the biggest impact.

3. *Two of your most important time blocks need to be for your personal Sabbath and date night with your spouse.* What doesn't get scheduled gets forgotten. Set aside these two important times first and then work everything else

around them. Your soul needs the Sabbath, and your marriage needs a weekly date night.

4. *Make sure the right people know what it is you've blocked time for.* If you have an assistant, keep him or her informed of when you have a block of time set aside for a certain project. He or she can run interference so you aren't interrupted. Also, let your spouse know when you won't be available. These important people can help you keep your time blocks intact.

5. *Give yourself a chance to make working in time blocks a habit.* If you are accustomed to jumping from one activity to another, or attempting to multitask, you may find it hard to devote so much focused time to a single task. Give yourself at least six weeks of blocking time to get used to it. That will allow you to develop the habit and become accustomed to this different—and better—way to work.

And here's a bonus tip to take you to the next level of time blocking:

6. *Group blocks of time for similar kinds of tasks, either on the same day or at around the same time of day on consecutive days.* For example, plan all of your writing—sermon outlines, Bible study outlines, books, and articles—for the morning hours every day. Or schedule all of your weekly meetings for a Tuesday. Doing this gives your brain a chance to lock in to similar activities and achieve a more intense level of focus.

Jumping from one task to another saps your energy and divides your focus. When you work in time blocks you multiply those invaluable resources and greatly increase your productivity. Put this easy time management tool to work for yourself right away.

Chapter 22

REMEMBER WHERE YOU LEFT OFF

Pastor Joe Average is in the middle of several big projects—projects large enough that they can't be completed in one sitting. Some of them will span months. There's just one problem: he tends to lose his place in the messy middle of such big projects. Then he wastes a lot of time trying to figure out where he left off when it's time to work on it again.

Pastor Rob Renegade stays organized, even in the midst of the many large projects he oversees. He can leave a project to go home and spend time with his family, then pick up right where he left off the next day, next week, or whenever the next scheduled time to work on it may be. As a result he gets things done more effectively. His congregation and his peers know him as a leader who accomplishes things—especially those big, important things.

A SIMPLE FIX TO A TIME-CONSUMING PROBLEM

Many tasks you will tackle will be small enough to complete in a single sitting. But for those larger projects you must always be able to track where you are. Many pastors waste a surprising amount of time looking for the place where they left off on such projects. This avoidable problem can waste a lot of time, but the fix is easy. It just takes a little intentionality.

To what kinds of projects does this apply? Really, anything that takes more than one block of time to finish or that involves more than one person. It could be something huge, like a building project, or a task that's far smaller but still important, like a sermon that will be delivered by more than one speaker. This also applies to overhaul projects that take long periods of time—like volunteer recruitment plans or the reorganization of children's ministries.

For any such project it is imperative that you know exactly where you left off when it's time to get back to work. You also need to know who is working on the different sections of the project, if applicable. If you neglect this important step, you will regret it. There are consequences to forgetting where you left off and trying to decide where to restart, such as:

- *Lost time.* Every minute spent trying to find your place is a minute of productivity lost. This can lead to the loss of momentum and even to missed project deadlines. In some cases a missed deadline on a big project means that additional money will have to be spent.

- *Lost confidence.* Searching for the place you stopped can erode not only your own confidence but also others' confidence in you. So much of leadership depends on your ability to inspire confidence. Don't give your staff or church members unnecessary reasons to doubt you.

- *Loss of reputation.* This is closely related to the previous point. You need to be a leader who has a reputation for efficiency and organization. When you can't find your starting place on a project, that's embarrassing. Your reputation takes a hit.

- *Duplicated work.* When you don't know where you left off, you run the risk of redoing something you've already completed. You also risk asking someone to do something that's either already been completed or already delegated to someone else. When that happens the people who are helping you get frustrated and lose motivation.

- *Lack of volunteers.* People are excited to take part in projects that will make an impact on others' lives. But they want to know their time isn't being wasted. When you can't find your place on a project, you come off looking disorganized. Volunteers are going to get discouraged and will be less likely to want to help you.

TIPS FOR EFFECTIVE PROJECT MARKING

You can no doubt see the benefits of making sure you mark where you left off on a project. This is a relatively simple step you must take for your own sake and for that of your reputation, your staff and volunteers, and your church. But what is the best way to do it? Here are three tips that will help you remember where you left off every time:

1. *Make a clear mark.* Whether you want to use a sticky note, draw a big red X, or something else, just be sure to clearly mark where you stopped working. Nondescript marks or enigmatic notations probably won't be helpful—they'll be easy for you to miss later on, and other people won't know what they mean.

2. *Let multiple people know where you are stopping.* Send an email to everyone who is helping you, letting them know the status of the project. That way, if one of them picks up working on it they'll know exactly where to start.

3. *Make sure everyone involved understands that this is an expected part of working on this project.* It takes only one person not marking his or her stopping place to make it hard for everyone else involved. Tell everyone that marking where they left off is required. No one is allowed to skip this important step.

And one bonus tip to help you make this part of your team's culture:

4. *Reward people who mark their ending spot consistently.* What gets rewarded gets repeated. When members of your team mark their spot, reward them in some way. Give them a gift card to a coffee shop or special recognition during your staff meeting. Just a small acknowledgment will get them on board, helping to make this practice a permanent part of your projects.

Clearly marking the place where you left off on a project seems like a small thing, but it will pay off in big ways. You will save yourself and those on your team a lot of time and frustration. Start making this a habit today.

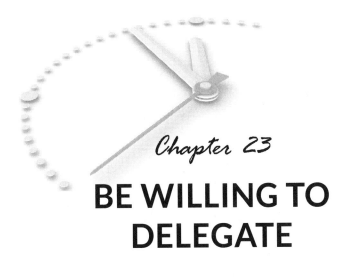

Chapter 23

BE WILLING TO DELEGATE

There's one question you, as a renegade pastor, should continually be asking yourself:

What am I doing that someone else could do just as well,
or nearly as well, as I do?

Pastors like to be in control. But the truth is that many of the activities you think you must do yourself could and should be handled by someone else. Learning to delegate to staff or reliable volunteers will free you up to accomplish the things that only you can do.

THE DIFFICULTIES OF DELEGATION

Proper delegation is key to every renegade pastor's ministry. In fact, it is so important that I (Nelson) have created an entire resource that teaches pastors how to delegate effectively (available at ChurchLeaderInsights.com). Yet delegation can be difficult for many reasons, including the following:

- *Pastors like to control things.* When you delegate to someone else, you can't always control what they are going to do.

- *Pastors are responsible.* Even if someone else is performing a task, you are ultimately responsible for making sure it's done well. This can cause you to believe that you would be better off just doing it yourself.

- *Pastors know what it feels like to be busy.* Since you understand all too well what it means to be truly busy, you may shy away from asking another busy person to add something to his or her to-do list.

THE BENEFITS OF DELEGATION

While the above concerns are valid, the benefits of delegation far outweigh them. In fact, proper delegation may be the single most effective tool God uses to expand and multiply your ministry. Why?

- *Delegation gives you time to plan and strategize.* Most of us would like more time to pray about and plan the future of our ministries. When you are willing to delegate you free up valuable time you can use to seek after God's vision for your ministry—something that, while not urgent, is vitally important. (See Chapter 4: Choose Important Over Urgent.)

- *Delegation builds trust within your congregation.* When you insist on doing everything yourself you send a clear signal that you don't trust the people around you. Delegation sends a different signal: that you are part of a team and you trust the people around you.

- *Delegation builds commitment among your congregation.* People who have a personal stake in what goes on in your church are going to be more committed. When you delegate you allow people to take ownership in the mission of the church—a critical step for discipleship. For more on this, see my (Nelson's) books, *Fusion: Turning First-Time Guests into Fully-Engaged Members of Your Church* and *Connect: How to Double Your Number of Volunteers.*

- *Delegation frees you to concentrate on what you are truly called to do.* God did not call you to pastor so you could file paperwork. When you delegate, you can focus on the big picture of what God wants you to do with your life and ministry.

- *Delegation may teach you a better way to do things.* Someone with a fresh perspective often approaches things in a way that might never have occurred to you. When you delegate you allow others to use their creativity to find more effective ways of operating.

- *Delegation builds other people's confidence and skills.* When you delegate, you allow others to develop skills they can use in every area of life. With those new skills comes the confidence that accompanies newfound competence.

HOW TO DELEGATE EFFECTIVELY

Given the benefits of effective delegation, it should be easy to see how delegating can make you and your church better. But … yes, it can still be hard to give up control. Here are six tips to help you get started:

1. *Be clear about what you expect.* It's easy to assume that someone else understands what you want done, simply because it's so clear to you. But when you delegate you must be sure to communicate, clearly and often, the expected outcome of the activity.

2. *Be clear about the limitations of a project.* Don't assume that everyone has the same moral or ethical code you do. Make sure the ground rules are clear to everyone involved, so they don't overstep a boundary they didn't know existed.

3. *Delegate according to people's interests, whenever possible.* People are far more likely to do a good job when they are working in an area they have an interest in. Assign people projects that correspond to their skills or passions.

4. *Stop expecting perfection.* The goal for most projects is to get it done, not to create a masterpiece. You need to be clear about your expectations, yes—but those expectations first need to be realistic. Excellence is achievable; perfection is not.

5. *Let every project become a teaching opportunity.* Most pastors are teachers at heart. Use that to your advantage. Teach people skills they may be lacking. Show them a better way when possible.

6. *Check on progress.* It isn't enough to give someone the responsibility to do something and to leave it at that. You need to to make sure that what you've asked has been understood and is being done. Checking in gives you an opportunity to keep people on task, as well as to motivate, teach, and encourage them.

And here is a bonus tip that may be more important than any of the others:

7. *Remember to say thank you!* These may be the two most important words in the English language. Always show your appreciation for a job well done.

God created the church so that his followers would have a place to come together for teaching, ministry, fellowship, worship and evangelism. And he doesn't expect you, as a pastor, to facilitate all of that alone.

Be sure to maximize the gifts, talents, and skills of the people he has strategically placed around you to help you accomplish his work. Delegate, delegate, delegate.

Chapter 24

MAKE THE MOST OF MEETINGS

The way you run meetings—your staff meetings in particular—says a lot about you as a leader. Do you get things started on time? Is there a clear, written agenda? Do you do a good job guiding the discussion and getting everyone involved? Do the meetings end on time? Do those in attendance know what they are expected to do before the next meeting?

While meetings may not be particularly fun, they are a necessary part of life in any organization. In fact, meetings are so important that I (Nelson) have a resource completely devoted to running effective meetings. (You can find it at ChurchLeaderInsights.com.) As a pastor, you have to meet with staff, with church members, and maybe even with members of your community. The way you are viewed as a leader will be determined in part by the manner in which you conduct these meetings. When you run organized, productive meetings, both your reputation and your productivity will skyrocket.

BAD MEETING BLUES

People don't like meetings largely because most of them are run so badly. Following are some telltale signs of a bad meeting:

- *They start late.* When you start a meeting late, you send the signal that the meeting isn't important and neither is the time of everyone involved. Plus, no matter the reason, starting late always leaves you looking unprepared.

- *There is no clear agenda.* A clear, written agenda is vital to any meeting. With no agenda, no one knows what's going to be discussed. This raises the level of stress for everyone in the room. No one likes surprises—not in this context, anyway.

- *There is no direction to the discussion.* Every meeting is made up of people who are more outspoken and others who are quieter. Unless there is clear direction, meetings can be dominated by the extroverted personalities in the room, while the valuable input of the introverts gets overlooked.

- *They run long.* We have all been to meetings that were supposed to end at a certain time but stretched later. This shows a clear disrespect for the time of everyone involved. Every person sitting in that meeting has a busy schedule. With every minute that ticks by it is likely that some of them are becoming later and later for another commitment.

When meetings are run badly, the leader comes off looking poorly prepared and disrespectful. Participants will assume the leader is disorganized, or at a minimum careless with the time, energy and commitments of others. Whether or not these perceptions are valid, none of them lends itself well to a healthy, effective organization.

RUNNING MEETINGS RENEGADE-STYLE

As a renegade pastor you can learn to conduct meetings that they are positive experiences. They still may not be particularly fun and exciting; that's just the nature of meetings. But they can be organized, productive, and beneficial to everyone involved. Here are five keys to making meetings better:

1. *Decide whether the meeting is even necessary.* Too many meetings don't need to happen. If a matter can be handled via a conference call or a couple of emails, it is better to spare everyone the time and trouble of getting together. Make sure to schedule meetings only when they are necessary and make certain to limit the discussion to items that affect everyone in attendance.

2. *Set a clear agenda.* Don't start a meeting without knowing exactly what you need to discuss and decide. Provide a written agenda to make the purpose of the meeting clear to those in attendance. This will help everyone stay on topic. When someone goes off on a tangent, having a clear agenda will allow you to steer the conversation back to the issues at hand.

3. *Let people know in advance what they need to prepare.* If there is some necessary reading to be done or if you will need a certain report during the meeting, be sure to make this clear beforehand. When people arrive at meetings prepared, everything goes more smoothly. Avoid surprising people with requests after the meeting has started.

4. *Get input from everyone.* Quiet people often get overlooked at meetings. Be careful to ensure that the stronger personalities aren't permitted to dominate.

5. *Provide clear next steps.* By the end of the meeting some action steps should be in place. Make sure that everyone knows what they need to do, and then hold them accountable.

Meetings are a great way to get the best minds in your church together to discuss issues that will make a difference in your ministry. Make sure you don't squander these opportunities by running bad meetings. When you take the necessary steps to make them pleasant and productive, meetings can go a long way toward advancing the vision and goals of your church.

Chapter 25

USE TECHNOLOGY WISELY

Technology is continuously changing the way we live—and mostly for the better. We no longer have to go to the bank and wait in line to make deposits or withdraw money. We have access to people at almost any time through our cellphones and email. We can find and catch up with old friends through social media sites. And these examples barely scrape the surface. With every passing year new technologies come along and our methods of doing things shift accordingly.

Technology makes us better connected and more productive and helps us in ministry. But it has drawbacks. Many average pastors get into trouble, losing precious time and energy, because they find themselves ensnared by the more dangerous aspects of our new, technology-driven world. Renegade pastors, on the other hand, acknowledge that technology is just a tool— something to be used for our benefit and God's glory.

THE PITFALLS OF TECHNOLOGY

God can and does use technology to accomplish tremendous good in the world. For example, I (Nelson) have been able to coach thousands of pastors and church leaders, helping them reach their God-given potential, largely because of advancements in technology. But it is easy to get off-track in this technological age. There's always a temptation to use technology in unproductive and even damaging ways. Following are a few of the downsides of too much technology:

- *Isolation.* Since it so easy to connect with people using text, email, and social media, you may find yourself neglecting personal interaction. God has called you to be out among the world. Despite technology, many interactions require a human, in-person touch.

- *Wasted time.* Have you ever opened social media with the intention of taking a quick look at what's going on, only to find yourself still scrolling and reading an hour later? While you can use those social media outlets for good—including the spread of the gospel—they can also eat away valuable time you will never get back.

- *Diminished physical fitness.* Sadly, obesity is the new normal in America—and Christians are one of the heaviest demographics. As I (Nelson) detail in my book *The Healthy Renegade Pastor*, poor physical health, far from honoring God, limits your ability to fulfill the purposes he put you on this earth to fulfill. Thanks largely to technology, people are becoming more sedentary than ever. God wants you and me to model a healthy, active lifestyle—and there are technologies out there that can help with that, if we will utilize them.

- *Temptation.* Pornography is a huge problem among Christians—even pastors. And it's available on any of our connected devices. Along with this, social media makes it easier than ever to connect with old romantic interests, potentially renewing relationships that shouldn't be rekindled. All of this can spell disaster for Christian leaders not on their guard.

- *Loss of reputation.* This can happen in many ways: an inappropriate post, a shared link that shouldn't have been shared, or even too many overtly political posts. Any of these actions can cause people to judge you in a negative light and possibly develop an undesirable view of your ministry.

- *Stress.* In many ways technology can ease the stress in your life. But the fact that you are always connected can also mean that you don't have the down time you need. True rest requires some disconnection.

USING TECHNOLOGY WISELY

With these potential pitfalls in mind, what's the best approach to engaging with today's ever-evolving technology? Some Christians think it's best to stay away from technology—especially social media—altogether. But we would argue that this would be a mistake for the renegade pastor. We are called to use every weapon at our disposal to advance God's Kingdom—and that certainly includes modern technology. The gospel is spread more effectively when you and I are willing to work with culture rather than fighting against it.

So, the question becomes: How can we use the tools of technology, and especially social media, to further God's Kingdom in our lives and ministries? Following are seven keys to using technology effectively:

1. *Set specific, personal time limits for your social media use.* Don't get sucked in to perusing social media sites for hours. Stick to a predetermined time limit. If necessary, set a timer.

2. *Dare to disconnect.* On your Sabbath day, try turning off both your phone and your computer. The world will still be spinning when you get back online. And your family

will appreciate the distraction-free time you have spent concentrating on them alone.

3. *Make exercise part of your daily routine.* Again, you were created to move. Don't get caught spending all day, every day, staring at your phone or computer. Get out. Walk. Bike with your kids. Move—and be healthier.

4. *Consider everything you do online to be public.* Don't say, post, or do anything online that you wouldn't be comfortable having your family and church view. Not long ago several pastors had to resign after a website devoted to helping people arrange extramarital affairs was hacked. It suddenly became public knowledge that these pastors had been active on that site. Not surprisingly, their lives and careers were ruined.

5. *Remember that God sees everything.* This is related to the point above. A good general rule is to not say anything online, or in a text or email, that isn't God-honoring. Enough said.

6. *Back up everything.* Have you ever lost important documents or contacts because your phone or computer crashed? Backup services are inexpensive and can spare you untold hours of lost time and worlds of heartache.

7. *Use technology to bring hope and healing.* There is far too much arguing, bashing, and negative talk online. Decide instead that you are going to use technology to spread hope and healing in Jesus' name.

Technology can be destructive. But in the hands of a wise renegade pastor it can also be a tool for tremendous good. Commit yourself to using technology to benefit others and bring God glory.

Chapter 26

MAKE PLANE TIME PRODUCTIVE TIME

Do you spend a lot of time on airplanes? Many pastors do. Whether it's traveling for conferences or flying halfway around the world to preach and build up local churches, air travel allows you and me to have a worldwide impact for God's Kingdom in a way that wasn't possible a couple of generations ago.

Like anything else, flying has its drawbacks. There's the hassle of getting to the airport and going through security, not to mention the possibility of lost luggage or other travel-related difficulties. But perhaps the biggest drawback is the downtime that is involved. There is so much waiting. Waiting in line. Waiting for your flight. Waiting to pick up your luggage. All on top of the time you spend sitting on the airplane to get where you are going. It's not unusual to end a day of travel feeling as though you have accomplished nothing other than getting from Point A to Point B. But air travel days don't have to be wasted days. With a little intentionality you can make sure they are productive days.

The time lost to traveling is time you'll never get back. That's why it's important to redeem as much of it as you can. Here are eight ways to make the most of your travel time:

1. *Get an aisle seat.* If possible, book an aisle seat. You will have more room, be more comfortable, and be able to

get to the restroom more easily. While none of these factors has a direct impact on your productivity, the more comfortable you are the more likely you will be able to focus and get some things done.

2. *Eat light.* Eating a heavy meal before boarding will inevitably leave you feeling groggy on the plane. Instead, eat lightly before the flight. You will have more energy to devote to your work.

3. *Use wait time to connect with people.* Have a list ready of people you need to call or text, and then check off as many as you can while you wait in the boarding area.

4. *Don't be afraid to nap.* Many pastors are consistently sleep-deprived. There is nothing wrong with using a portion of your flight to catch up on some sleep. Just remember that, in most cases, a forty-five-minute nap is all you need in order to feel refreshed. Any longer than that and you are likely to wake up feeling groggier than when you started your nap.

5. *Catch up on reading.* Make sure you have a few books with you. In fact, we recommend that you don't go anywhere without a book. You can take advantage of even small increments of downtime to catch up on a little reading.

6. *Take care of email or other small tasks.* You can respond to most emails in just a few minutes. So why not knock out a bunch of them while you fly? It will feel great to empty your inbox and take care of those small, nagging things you've been avoiding.

7. *Have a block of writing time.* It's best to write in blocks of time (see Chapter 21: Work in Blocks of Time). When you're on a plane, you'll have at least one ready-made

block of time. Plan to prepare a sermon, write a chapter of your book, or put together a Bible study.

8. *Think, pray, and dream.* Again, most pastors are too busy for their own good. They don't spend enough time just sitting and thinking strategically, looking for God's vision for their lives and ministries. Use flight time to take a step back and seek after God's heart for you.

Rather than viewing plane time as wasted time, start focusing on the opportunity it affords you to get some things accomplished that you otherwise wouldn't. For renegade pastors there is no such thing as wasted time. With the right mindset and preparation, time spent traveling can be time used for God's glory.

Chapter 27

TURN WAIT TIME INTO USEFUL TIME

We all spend more time waiting than we would like to. We wait on hold. We wait in line at the store. We wait for doctors' appointments. We wait for people who are late. Time spent waiting is frustrating, mostly because we see the time as wasted. But it doesn't need to be. That's average thinking. For renegade pastors every moment is redeemable—and you should seek to redeem every moment fully. When you do you can turn wait time into time that allows you to get some important things done.

But to begin utilizing wait time effectively you must first change the way you think about it. Instead of focusing on the frustration, look for the inherent opportunities. When you do, you'll see them everywhere. Your productivity level will jump so much, in fact, that you may end up wishing you had to wait more often!

WHAT TO DO WHILE YOU WAIT

What can you do while you wait? There are probably hundreds of answers to that question. Here are six that can help you be more productive immediately:

1. *Make phone calls.* Unless you are waiting on the phone, you can make calls while you wait. You should always

have at your disposal a list of people you need to contact. Tackle that list while you wait for something else to happen.

2. *Review your calendar.* As a renegade pastor, you schedule everything on your calendar. Keeping that calendar clean and uncluttered may take a little maintenance. Use your waiting moments to make sure it is up-to-date and in order.

3. *Sort and respond to email.* Even if you have only a few minutes of wait time, you can use it to respond to email. There's never a shortage of messages that need attention, right?

4. *Organize your day.* This is an especially good idea if you find yourself waiting early in the day. Use your wait time to think through your day, and even your week, with a mind toward maximum effectiveness.

5. *Relax.* Occasionally you just need to exhale. Maybe God put you in a holding pattern so you could take a quick break. Breathe deeply, let your mind wander freely, and trust that God is in control—even when you find yourself standing in the slowest line in the store.

6. *Talk with a stranger.* You never know whom you might meet in line at the post office or in an airport lobby. Strike up a conversation with someone you don't know. God might use you to be a blessing in that person's life— or perhaps even vice versa.

Here is a bonus idea that renegade pastors can use to make wait time more productive:

7. *Get familiar with the features on your phone.* You likely have a smartphone that can do amazing things—things that could save you a huge amount of time and energy. While you wait, teach yourself how to use some of these underutilized time-saving features.

Waiting is a part of life. Instead of falling into the trap of viewing it as wasted time, make sure you adopt the renegade pastor's mindset. Look for the opportunities to turn wait time into productive time. Soon you will be getting more accomplished than you would have ever thought possible. When used well, wait time can be time for you to enlarge your ministry and improve your life.

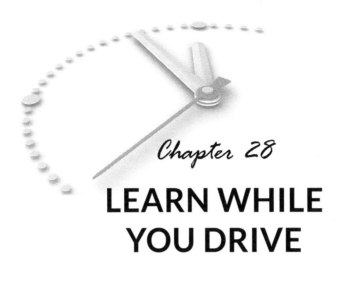

Chapter 28

LEARN WHILE YOU DRIVE

Imagine riding to work every day with the pastors of some of the most successful churches in the world or with top business leaders in any given field. Just think of the nuggets they would drop, the wisdom they could impart, on those drives. Think of the tips you'd pick up that could revolutionize your ministry—and even your life. You could listen to them reflect on what they had done right and the mistakes they had made, hopefully preventing you from making the same ones. You would learn so much in your car every day before even getting to work. Wouldn't that be an incredible opportunity?

The truth is that you can! Podcasts and audiobooks give you the opportunity to access the wisdom of leaders in nearly every field. They allow you to hear from some of the brightest minds on the planet, at your convenience. Declining to take advantage of the opportunity to travel with and learn from such mentors is a mistake too many average pastors make.

NEVER STOP LEARNING

Leaders are lifelong learners. In fact, it is very dangerous for a leader to stop learning. You may be okay for a while, getting by on your intelligence, your prior knowledge or previous experiences, or your reputation as a leader. But eventually a lack of learning will catch up with you. It will limit your fruitfulness as a pastor and your effectiveness in daily life. When you stop learning, in fact, you might as well stop leading. You'll first begin to stagnate and then find yourself slipping backward in ways that are so subtle you may not even notice until it's too late.

Continually filling your mind with fresh ideas and truths from those with different and more experiences is keeps you moving forward. Audio recordings give you an easy opportunity to do just that. You can grow your skills, gain new insights, and even deepen your walk with God—all while you drive to and from work.

TAKE ADVANTAGE OF DRIVING TIME

In addition to continuing your education, there is another good reason to listen to audio recordings while you drive. When you listen and learn, you are redeeming what would otherwise be wasted time. Often driving time is written off as nothing more than what it seems to be—a necessity to get you where you are going. But driving time can be extremely valuable, if you will choose to use it for your good. You can spend that unavoidable time behind the wheel gaining knowledge, soaking in wisdom, and deepening your faith.

So take the world's great minds with you everywhere you go. It doesn't matter whether you download podcasts to your phone, listen to audiobooks, or use CDs or any other audio medium. Just choose whatever method makes you comfortable and dig in. There's no wrong way to do it. Keep a few ideas in mind as you begin to explore some of the great wisdom that is available to you through audio teaching:

1. *Subscribe to your favorite podcasts, so they will come to you automatically.* When you subscribe to a podcast you don't have to remember to retrieve it. It comes to you

without any effort on your part. And subscribing is easy from any one of several apps on your smartphone.

2. *Listen to leaders in areas outside of Christian ministry.* It is easy to get caught up in listening solely to people talking about ministry. But you can also learn a great deal from those with expertise in other areas. Take advantage of the wide range of the teaching that's available to you.

3. *Use podcasts to strengthen your faith.* Not every podcast is informational. Many are devotional in nature and can greatly enrich your walk with God. Make it a point to listen to recordings that feed your heart as well as your head.

4. *Listen to non-Christian podcasts and audiobooks.* For pastors there is value in understanding what unbelievers think and care about, in learning about the culture around you. Non-Christian podcasts and audiobooks give you an opportunity to do just that.

Renegade pastors know how to make any time useful time. The time you spend driving doesn't need to be wasted. Make it productive by taking advantage of great audiobooks and podcasts. Keep learning, keep growing, and keep reaching to become the person and pastor God has called you to be.

Chapter 29

TRADE MONEY FOR TIME

People look to you for so many things—for leadership, guidance, counseling, vision-casting, and theology, just to name a few. Yet while you are smart and competent, you are also human. There are limits to what you can do, many of which are simply the result of limited time. Every day you are bound by the same twenty-four hours, and there is always more that needs to be done in those hours than is realistically possible.

Again, part of using your time wisely involves setting good priorities. What are the things you must do, that can't be delegated? What are the things someone else could do if you would allow them to? When you begin to step back and address these questions thoughtfully, you will inevitably see that there are many things on your plate that you can delegate to others. (See Chapter 23: Be Willing to Delegate.)

PAYING FOR TIME AND EXPERTISE

There are certain tasks that can be effectively accomplished by someone else, but getting them done will cost you a little money. Secular companies do this all the time—they spend money to save time and enable them to concentrate on their priorities. You should, too. For a small fee you can outsource many small tasks to others and save yourself valuable time that you can use to accomplish more for your family and for God's Kingdom.

In your particular case, this approach to maximizing your time may be a bit controversial. After all, it will cost you or your church some money. And most pastors and churches don't have extra money lying around. But the benefits of trading money for time can make a lot of sense in many instances. There are two major benefits to this time-saving approach:

- *It helps you save the most precious resource you have—time.* No matter how rich or intelligent you are, once a minute is gone you can never get it back. On the other hand, you can always make more money. So doesn't it make sense in many cases to forgo something less precious (money) in order to gain something more precious (time)?

- *It helps you concentrate on the work God has called you to do.* The activities you outsource to others should be things that aren't directly related to the tasks God has given you or your church. By hiring someone else to take care of trivial but necessary activities, you free yourself to focus on more essential things.

What kinds of activities can you outsource for a fee? There are dozens, but here are four to consider. Pay someone to take these time-consuming tasks off your plate and free up time that can be better spent elsewhere.

1. *Hire a virtual assistant to handle email and other small activities.* This is especially helpful if you don't have a church secretary to handle these matters. A virtual assistant can read emails, flag the important ones for you to respond to, and even respond to some of them on your

behalf. This can be a huge timesaver. And virtual assistants aren't usually terribly expensive. In addition, you may want to use this person to schedule meetings or take care of other small administrative tasks on your behalf.

2. *Hire someone to handle marketing and publicity for your church.* Whether you call it marketing or outreach, you must let your community know who you are and what you have to offer. Hire someone to draft press releases and design postcards or invitations. You may also want to hire someone to design graphics, such as a church logo. I (Richard) hired a graphic designer to design my church's logo for about fifty dollars. She designed an incredible logo that has served us very well—definitely worth the minimal investment.

3. *Hire someone to mow your lawn and do your landscaping.* Of course you can mow your own lawn—but is this the best use of your time? Is it what you should be doing when you have a few minutes away from the church? Or could that time be better spent with your family, recharging, or doing something else for God's Kingdom? Again, time is more precious than money.

4. *Hire someone to do your grocery shopping.* I (Richard) have used a grocery shopping service from time to time, when my wife and I have been busier than usual. I pay a small fee for the service and end up saving two or three hours of combined shopping and driving time. I have found this to be a worthwhile tradeoff.

Trading money for time is a key principle for renegade pastors to consider, but there are a few cautions to keep in mind:

- *Privacy and security.* If you are giving someone your email password, or any kind of personal information, make certain they are trustworthy. Anyone you hire should be able to provide you with references—which you should check. In addition, most reputable agencies will carry insurance and check the references of the virtual assistants they recommend.

- *Budget concerns.* Keep your budget in mind when hiring someone. Don't spend money you don't have, just to save time. Don't acquire any debt. But do make the money-for-time trade whenever you can.

- *Supervise.* Even when you give a job to someone else, the ultimate responsibility for getting it accomplished still belongs to you. Always ask for a report on what a virtual assistant has done. Set benchmarks for writers or graphic designers to meet. If something isn't being done to your satisfaction, find someone else to do the job.

For some people the concept of trading money for time is new. It may take some getting used to. That said, this principle can be extremely effective in helping you accomplish more of what God has called you to do. Think about what you might be able to achieve if you were to put this concept to work in your life—and then take a few small steps toward trading money for time.

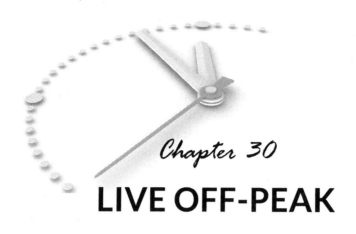

Chapter 30

LIVE OFF-PEAK

The Sunday lunch rush is a real phenomenon. Churchgoers joke with each other about hoping to get out of the service in time to beat the lunch rush—that period, just after all the churches around town let out, when every restaurant is filled with local Christians. If you have ever been a part of the Sunday lunch rush you know exactly what it means: a long wait to be seated, followed by another lengthy wait for food.

And pastors need to eat, too, right? A few years ago my wife and I (Richard) figured out that if we were to stall until about two o'clock on Sunday afternoons we could avoid getting tangled up in the crowds of people and the prolonged wait times. So, I have made a habit of doing some follow-up work for about an hour after our service ends. Then, we go to lunch when the rush is over.

OFF-PEAK LIVING

This small adjustment is a great example of one of the best time-management principles out there: living off-peak. The idea is simple, but the effect on your life can be profound. You can literally shave off an hour or more of wasted minutes each week simply by adjusting your schedule so that you do things at a time when everyone else is doing something else.

The reason living off-peak works so well is simple: human beings are creatures of habit. People do the same things at the same times of the day, week in and week out. And when a lot of people decide to do the same thing at the same time it creates lines, delays, and the potential for a lot of frustration and wasted time. But renegade pastors don't waste time—they maximize it.

Lots of people go to the bank on Friday afternoons. Many people frequent home-improvement stores on weekend mornings. And grocery stores are typically packed after work with people stopping by for an item or two on their way home. These patterns are predictable—which means that you can take note of them and decide to do the same things at different times. One of the advantages of being a pastor is that your schedule has a little more flexibility than that of many people, allowing you to be intentional about taking care of your routine tasks at off-peak times.

Not only will you save time by living off-peak, but you will experience something that is equally important: a decrease in your level of frustration. Being a pastor, as you know too well, can be frustrating even under the best of circumstances. When you add the irritation of standing in long lines and fighting traffic and in-store crowds, your stress level can elevate quickly. Living off-peak gets you out of those situations and increases your peace of mind.

DECIDING TO DO THINGS DIFFERENTLY

The key to living off-peak is making the decision to do things differently—which is what being a renegade pastor is all about. The easy way, the average way, is to do things in the same way and at the same times everyone else is doing them. You, however, have abandoned average. Following are a few considerations that can help you make the change to off-peak living:

1. *Different areas have different peak times.* In resort or tourist-heavy locales you might see earlier mealtime rushes, whereas in major cities the dinner rush probably happens later in the evening. Get to know your area so you can pinpoint the peak times you want to avoid.

2. *Combine off-peak errands whenever possible.* Go to the bank, shop for groceries, and do other similar errands during the afternoon hours, when other people are chained to their desks. You will realize a savings in driving time alone when you do several similar things in a single time block.

3. *Skip going out altogether by automating.* To save valuable time, automate everything you possibly can, from paying utility bills to grocery shopping. (For more on automating, see Chapter 12: Automate as Much as Possible.)

4. *Look for off-peak discounts.* This is a great way to save money and time. Many places, such as movie theaters and some restaurants, offer discounts and lower prices for people who use their services at unusual times. Take advantage of the discounts when you can and keep some more money in your pocket.

Living off-peak is a great, simple way to save time. Every minute you save by not being stuck in traffic, not waiting in line, or not waiting for a table, is a minute you can spend on ministry. So start living off-peak today.

POSTSCRIPT

We hope this book will become a conversation starter between us. We are continually developing resources and gathering ideas to help you abandon average and fully live the Renegade Pastor lifestyle. Let's stay in touch, either indirectly, through your subscription to my free newsletter, or directly, as you officially join the Renegade Pastors Network. Find out about both at this book's website:

www.RenegadePastorsTimeManagement.com

You can also use the website to connect with me personally. I would love to hear your story and to continue discussing ways in which we can grow together for God's glory.

Your partner in ministry,

Nelson Searcy
Lead Pastor, The Journey Church
Lead "Renegade Pastor,"
www.RenegadePastors.com

Richard Jarman
Lead Pastor, TouchPoint Church
Bell Gardens, CA
Member, Renegade Pastors Network

ACKNOWLEDGMENTS

Nelson Searcy: First and foremost, I would like to thank Jesus Christ for the opportunity to serve his church. I would also like to thank my co-author on this book. This is my first book with Richard Jarman although we have worked on many smaller projects prior. His commitment to abandon average in his life and ministry is a testimony to all of us "Renegade Pastors." Thank you, Richard, for your friendship, influence and passion — and especially for your willingness to model the Renegade Pastor's Time Management lifestyle.

I must also express my appreciation to the staff and members of The Journey Church; the alumni from my coaching networks who shared their testimonies and assisted in the ideas developed in this book; and the entire team at Church Leader Insights, especially Sandra Olivieri (who shepherded this project from beginning to end) plus thanks to Seth Stone and Jimmy Britt. Thanks to my writing partner, Jennifer Dykes Henson, for her time to make copy edits on this book even while we were under a tight deadline for another project. And thank you to Donna Huisjen for her keen eye and invaluable editorial input.

My passion for a renegade approach to time management is first and foremost about obedience to scripture and my intention to fulfill God's call upon my life. But a close second to that is my desire to honor my marriage to Kelley and to be a God-honoring parent to my son, Alexander — I love you both! Now, off to my dentist appointment, the first one after lunch ... living off-peak!

Richard Jarman: I give thanks, first of all, to Jesus Christ, who saved me, and allows me to serve as pastor of TouchPoint Church, the greatest church in the world. Every minute of life I have is a gift from Him. Thank you Lord for the ability to use this gift of time!

Thanks also goes to Nelson Searcy, who has been a friend and mentor for a number of years. I love what you and the CLI team do to instruct and encourage pastors! You and your family our continually in my prayers.

I am also grateful for TouchPoint Church in Bell Gardens, California, where I am privileged to serve. God has put us on a wonderful journey together, serving Him by serving our city. You all love me, and challenge me to be all Jesus wants me to be. Thank you!

Thank you to my kids: Samuel, Grace, Abigail, Joseph, and Hope. I love you! I am so proud of each of you. I can't wait to see what God has in store for you. And, especially, my wife, Jennifer. My love for you grows with every day. I am so blessed to be able to spend this crazy life with you!

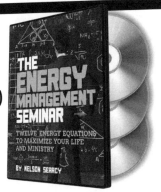

ADDITIONAL BOOKS
BY NELSON SEARCY:

Launch: Starting a New Church From Scratch
Topic: Church Planting

The Difference Maker: Using Your Everyday Life For Eternal Impact
Topics: Evangelism, Spiritual Growth

The Renegade Pastor: Abandoning Average in Your Life and Ministry
Topic: Leadership

Maximize: How to Develop Extravagant Givers in Your Church
Topic: Stewardship

Connect: How to Double Your Number of Volunteers
Topic: Ministry

Engage: A Guide to Creating Life-Transforming Worship Services
Topic: Worship Planning

Fusion: Turning First-Time Guests Into Fully-Engaged Members of Your Church
Topic: Assimilation

The Healthy Renegade Pastor: Abandoning Average in Your Health and Wellness
Topics: Leadership, Health

Tongue Pierced: How the Words You Speak Transform the Life You Live
Topic: Leadership

Ignite: How to Spark Immediate Growth in Your Church
Topics: Growth Barriers, Evangelism

The Generosity Ladder: Your Next Step to Financial Peace
Topic: Stewardship

The Greatness Principle: Finding Significance and Joy by Serving Others
Topic: Ministry

Revolve: A New Way to See Worship
Topic: Worship Planning

Activate: An Entirely New Approach to Small Groups
Topic: Small Groups

These books are available at www.Amazon.com and www.ChristianBook.com
For other resources, visit our websites:

www.ChurchLeaderInsights.com
www.RenegadePastors.com

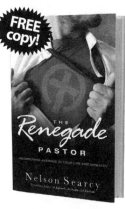

WHEN AVERAGE ISN'T GOOD ENOUGH ANYMORE...

Join the Renegade Pastors Network now – only $1.00 for two months (a $198.00 value)! Plus, get a FREE book — the first in the Renegade series — and $895.45 in FREE RESOURCES!

FREE MEMBER BONUSES!

In addition to your Renegade Pastor book ($19.95 value), you'll immediately receive **$895.45 in FREE bonus resources hand-picked by Nelson!**

You get all of these resources!

The Renegade Pastors Network is so much more than these resources: it's about a comprehensive approach to life and ministry.

Here's what's waiting for you in the Renegade Pastors Network:

- **A monthly Leadership Briefing Call** with Nelson where you'll be challenged and guided to maximize your ministry each month.

- **A monthly Equipping Interview Call**, where Nelson interviews other leading authors – past interviews include Patrick Lencioni, Larry Osborne and Gary McIntosh.

- **MP3 recordings of both the briefing and interview calls each month** — don't worry if you can't make the live calls, you won't miss a thing.

- **Members-Only Online Hub** where you can access your files, resources and recordings at all times.

- **Membership Welcome Kit** upon joining with resources and bonuses so you can immediately start abandoning average!

- **Mailed Monthly Members Update** with 16+ page printed Renegade Pastors Insider, in-depth book summaries, Church Growth Champions reports and more!

- And much more!

Are you ready to go Renegade?
Sign up today for only $1.00:
www.RenegadePastors.com/onedollar

How HEALTHY is Your Church?

Get a FREE COPY of Nelson Searcy's Revised & Expanded *8 Systems of a Healthy Church* e-book! ($23.95 value)

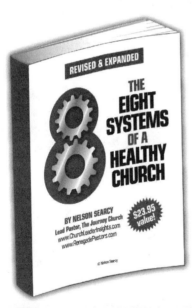

God designed all the parts of the body – both the church body and the physical body – to work together, allowing us to fulfill his purposes and plans on this earth. And both of those respective bodies function best through well-developed systems.

Nelson Searcy's revised & expanded *8 Systems of a Healthy Church* e-book has been updated with new chapters for Assimilation and Stewardship. Learn from pastors who have been using the systems in their own churches. Get practical help as you lead your church to greater health and effectiveness.